SPOR

Happy

CROSSING THE LINE

How Australian cricket lost its way

GIDEON HAIGH

slattery
MEDIA GROUP

www.slatterymedia.com

The Slattery Media Group Pty Ltd
Level 39/385 Bourke Street, Melbourne
Victoria, Australia, 3000

Text © Gideon Haigh, 2018
Design © The Slattery Media Group Pty Ltd, 2018
Published by The Slattery Media Group, 2018

All rights reserved. No part of this publication may be reproduced, stored in a
retrieval system or transmitted in any form or by any means without the prior written
permission of the copyright owner. Inquiries should be made to the publisher.
Inquiries should be made to the publisher.

A catalogue record for this
book is available from the
National Library of Australia

Group Publisher: Geoff Slattery
Editor: Russell Jackson
General and project manager: Jeffrey Sickert
Art Direction, Cover Design and Typeset: Kate Slattery

Printed in Australia by Griffin Press
slatterymedia.com

CROSSING THE LINE

How Australian cricket lost its way

ESSAYS ABOUT REMARKABLE SPORTSPEOPLE & MEMORABLE EVENTS

Crossing the Line is the first of Slattery Media Group's *Sports Shorts* collection, a new home for lively and engaging writing on sport. Every instalment will illuminate or entertain, all the while fitting into your back pocket on the way to the game.

Contents

Something Afoot

At 3pm on 24 March, 2018, South Africa led Australia in the Third Test at Cape Town's Newlands Stadium by 185 runs with eight second-innings wickets in hand. Aiden Markram and AB de Villiers had settled comfortably; the bowlers, at the back end of a long summer, were wearying; the ball, more than 40 overs old, was aloof from efforts to make it swing or seam.

Cutting from face to face in the Australian ring, television cameras captured grim expressions, accentuated by the gloom. The series scoreline stood at one-all, Australia's win at Kingsmead having been cancelled out by South Africa's at St George's Park. But on the field, parity had long slid away. When umpires Nigel Llong and Richard Illingworth beckoned, Australia's Cameron Bancroft and captain Steve Smith hurried to their side, the sense was of deepening embattlement. *Cricinfo's* ball-by-ball commentator clicked alertly into bold: "They are having a chat with Cameron Bancroft, and **there could be something afoot here**."

The umpires were responding to advice from their off-field colleague Ian Gould. Production staff at broadcaster *SuperSport* had rewound earlier vision of Bancroft rubbing one side of the ball with a conspicuously cupped right hand, before ostentatiously shining the other side on the back of his trousers. During the countries' preceding two series, it had been Australians who had noised suspicion about the South Africans' doctoring of the condition of the Kookaburra ball. Now the Australians were under scrutiny and knew it full well. Cameras had trailed Smith's vice-captain David Warner, the team's deputed ball 'maintenance man', throughout the tour, commentators at St George's commenting on his heavily bandaged right hand. With Warner less obviously active in this innings, they had shifted their gaze to twenty-five-year-old Bancroft, suddenly conspicuously busy. His hands were bare, so the umpires enquired about the contents of his pockets, from which he nervously produced an item of cloth—apparently a sleeve for the sunglasses perched backwards on his baggy green. Having examined the ball,

Long and Illingworth threw it back. When the exchange ended, *Cricinfo's* commentator promised more: "Will elaborate if needs be!" Elaboration was not long coming.

C ricket has never quite been able to make up its mind about 'ball tampering'—the deliberate degrading of the ball to create a surface aerodynamically conducive to reverse swing, sharper and later than the conventional variety. Throw the ball into a naturally occurring abrasive surface like rough soil on a pitch square, and that seems okay providing you don't do it too obviously; apply a naturally occurring abrasive instrument—like a fingernail—and you're beyond the bounds. Ballasting a ball with saliva is condoned; stimulating or sweetening that saliva with a lolly or jube is not, at least if you're caught at it. Historically, the penalty has been a mere five runs— the same incurred when a ball strikes an unused helmet. Ethically, offences have taken on a darker complexion— in 2006, a ball tampering accusation led to Pakistan's forfeiture of an Oval Test match. Some, regarding reverse swing as a skill, have called for its legalisation, noting that overarm bowling was once beyond the pale; others have espoused zero tolerance, including Australia. "We hold our heads high and I'll be very disappointed if one of our team members did that," Warner once said.

Most accusations of ball tampering are illustrated by blurry photos of cricket balls with prying fingers in proximity to the seam; most charges of misbehaviour contain some degree of ambiguity, the mitigation hot temper or severe provocation. None of these applied at Newlands. When Bancroft peeled away from the umpires, the footage of his two-part ball handling routine played across Newlands' giant video screen, amid murmurs, mumblings, heckles and boos. The camera was then trained on the Australians' open-fronted dressing room. Earlier in the tour, Darren Lehmann had offered a smirking response to questions about Australian methods of ball preparation: "Obviously there's techniques used by both sides to get the ball reversing. That's just the way the game goes. I have no problem with it. Simple." Now the coach looked confused, hesitant. He contacted 12th man Peter Handscomb in the dugout to ask what was going on. In the meantime, fiddling self-consciously with the waistband, Bancroft withdrew a small yellow object from his right-hand pocket and dropped it down the front of his pants.

S ometimes on the cricket field, things are not as they seem. Sometimes replays enlarge, exaggerate, mislead. Usually a note of caution will be sounded: let us hear what they, the players, have to say. This was not one of those occasions. Through the day's last hour, before it was curtailed by bad light with South Africa nearly 300 to the good, still with five wickets in reserve, the footage was analysed and analysed, each time looking more crass than the last. Commentators Allan Border ("very suspicious"), Graeme Smith ("quite damning") and Shane Warne ("we've got to get to the bottom of it") were of a mind. As responses crackled across social media, the tones were of horror and indignation. Australian team manager Gavin Dovey knocked on the door of the match referee Andy Pycroft: yes, he was advised, Bancroft would be charged with breaching clause 41.3 of the International Cricket Council's playing conditions, for changing the ball's condition with an 'artificial substance', with a hearing to occur when the match concluded.

As the Australians huddled in their dressing room, there were more immediate concerns. A Test match and a series had tilted decisively that day, but all anyone wanted to know about was the footage of Bancroft and that yellow object. Precisely what transpired in the next twenty minutes may never be known, even if multiple versions are bound to emerge. There was a ragged form of inquest: yes, Bancroft had applied sandpaper to the ball; yes, Warner had been the instigator; yes, Smith had acquiesced in it. The conversation drew in Lehmann, Dovey, assistant coach David Saker, team psychologist Michael Lloyd and public affairs manager Kate Hutchison, who was in touch with her boss Tim Whittaker in Melbourne. The immediate issue was who should front the nightly media conference. The umpires, it was noted, had not changed the ball; the charges were being prepared by Gould and by fourth umpire Allahudien Paleker. But when a huddle formed around an analyst's laptop to study the footage, there was no denying its grossness.

Bizarrely, nobody was obviously in charge. Obedient, self-sacrificing, Bancroft was prepared to cop to it. But would that prejudice the disciplinary action against him? The coaches offered little. The public affairs staff were leery. Dovey, who has a law degree, was concerned that nobody seemed completely clear what they should say, if they said anything. He tried to ring his boss Pat Howard, but, in the early hours of the morning in Brisbane, Cricket Australia's executive general manager, team performance, was asleep; so, in Melbourne, was chief executive officer James Sutherland. The players, accustomed to writing the past off and tackling the next challenge, were more pragmatic. They were involved in a Test match with two days to play. Consensus emerged that they should simply 'get it out of the way'.

Fifteen months earlier, at a previous low point in his captaincy, a gruesome Test defeat at Bellerive Oval, Smith had been widely praised for his candour with the press ("I'm embarrassed to be sitting here, to be perfectly honest"), and come to view it in hindsight as "the making of me as a captain", giving him "confidence to know I was capable of dealing with whatever the job could throw at me." Fifteen years earlier, Lehmann had been involved in an incident in a one-day international against Sri Lanka, where he responded to dismissal with a notorious racist expletive: "Black cunts". He had elected to front the media immediately—a public relations strategy known as 'confess and avoid'. "The idea behind the approach is to get all the bad news out into the open as quickly as possible so that the story, with no new angles to feed off, runs out of legs," Lehmann explained. "It worked out as well as it could have done for me in the circumstances." After a five-match suspension he worked his passage back in a World Cup. Among a range of bad options, confession and avoidance now seemed to Smith and Bancroft the least worst.

As Hutchison ushered the players into the media conference area, they still wore their baggy greens, tugged over faces streaked with sunscreen. That patina of purpose quickly wore off. As the first question was asked, Smith's eyes swivelled to Bancroft. "Want to explain?" said the Australian captain, with the inference that he did not. Not surprisingly, Bancroft faltered over his response. "Yeah look, we had a discussion during the break," he said. "And on myself I saw an opportunity to use some tape, get some granules from, y'know, the rough patches on the wicket, and try to, I guess, to change the ball condition. It didn't work. The umpires didn't change the ball. But I guess, y'know, once being sighted on the screen and having done that I panicked quite a lot and that obviously resulted in me shoving it down, umm, down my trousers." Some nervous laughter escaped the audience.

So, the foreign object was "tape"? Bancroft again stumbled: "Yeah, we have this yellow tape in our kit and it is connected to actually some padding but the actual sticky stuff is very sticky and I felt, yeah, like it could be used to collect some stuff from the side of the pitch."

So, who was "we"? Smith was about to make this clear— and not: "Yeah, the leadership knew about it, we spoke about it at lunch." Solemn sigh. "I'm not proud of what's happened. Y'know, it's not within the spirit of the game. My integrity, the team's integrity, the leadership group's integrity, has come into question and rightfully so. It's not on. It's certainly not on and it won't happen again, I can promise you that, under my leadership."

The more Smith strove for candour, the less he somehow achieved it. "It was the leadership group," he reiterated. "I'm not naming names but the leadership group were what talked about it and Bangers [Bancroft] was around at the time and we spoke about it and thought it was a possible way to get an advantage, and, ummm, obviously it didn't work, the umpires didn't see it change the, ummm, the way the ball was behaving, or how it looked or anything like that." Smith shook his head wearily: "So, poor choice and deeply regrettable, umm, I guess, our actions."

From bad it deteriorated. Every reply Smith offered seemed to call forth half a dozen further questions, which he proved ever less able to answer. No, he had not spoken to anyone in Australia. No, the coaches were not involved. No, the action was isolated. A trace of exasperation entered Smith's voice: "You can ask questions as much as you like but I can promise you this is the first time it's happened and I think I've made it clear, we're regrettable and we'll move on from this. Hopefully we'll learn something from it. I'm embarrassed, I know the boys in the shed are embarrassed as well, and I feel for Cam as well. It's not what we want to see in the game, it's not what the Australian cricket team's about, and being the leader of the team I'm, umm, incredibly sorry for, I guess, trying to bring the game into disrepute like we did today."

For the gravest question at least, his answer was unequivocal: "No, I won't be considering stepping down. I still think I'm the right the person for the job. Obviously, today was a big mistake on my behalf and on the leadership group's behalf as well. But I take responsibility as the captain, I need to take control of the ship, but this is certainly something I'm not proud of and something that I can hope to learn from and come back strong from." In fact, he was making his final public remarks as Australian captain.

E ven now, months after the event, the omnishambles of Newlands seems hard to believe. Australia's cricketers have been seen in various shades down the decades—brave and defiant; austere and uncompromising; overweening and confrontational. The last guise had been a feature of the South African tour, with Warner, as often, the principal, swaggering antagonist. Yet here they were in fresh and uniquely unflattering lights: sneaky, furtive, oblivious and dim. A conflagration of criticism consumed every atom of media oxygen on a slow news Sunday.

The captain's a cheat! They threw the kid under the bus! The coaches must have known!

Retribution was swift. Investigation established that Bancroft's talk of granulated "sticky tape" and Smith's of the "leadership group" at the press conference were economies on the truth, and suspensions were levelled accordingly: twelve months on Smith and Warner, nine months on Bancroft. Lehmann was a casualty; Cricket Australia has since parted company with its chief executive, most distinguished director and most experienced legal officer, not to mention the public affairs manager Hutchison. Individuals and institution were abandoned by a drove of sponsors; it remains to be seen how many disenchanted fans have decided likewise.

Yet there remains a sense that we do not quite know all there is to know. That full knowledge of Australian ball maintenance was confined to just three individuals stretches credulity. Modern cricket teams devote immense effort to expediting reverse swing—in part a necessary response to the growing dominion of the bulked-up, dried-out bat, and the uneven quality of the proud-seamed, machine-stitched ball, of which a new one comes from each end in one-day internationals. Rumours circulate of sandpaper's use in less-vigilant domestic T20 leagues. Whatever the case, the only taboo is on getting caught. Australian cricket is no stranger to cover-ups and/

or non-looks. Suspicion lingers that there remains more to say, although it may as yet be a little soon: it took four years for Mark Waugh and Shane Warne to have to admit, most unwillingly, to tarrying with bookmakers; a decade elapsed before referee Mike Procter shared his version of the fiasco that was Monkeygate.

Crossing the Line originates in a simpler idea, that nobody goes to sleep honest and wakes up a cheat. The drift to corruption occurs little by little, influenced by example, precedent, incentive and human material, and after a time may need a third party to identify it as such. Lurking behind events at Newlands is a disturbing counterfactual. What if *SuperSport*'s cameramen had not been so attentive? What if Bancroft had not panicked? Where would the cheating have bottomed? What if anything would have arrested it?

An irony is that what transpired in Newlands also acted to save a few blushes, continuing what has been by some measures Australia's bleakest cricket decade since the eighties, at least away from home. Since Australia was toppled from its perch atop the Test rankings in August 2009, it has lost more than half its Tests abroad (27 of 51) and won fewer than half its one-day internationals (63 of 128). A team good enough to secure a World Cup and regain the Ashes on its own shores becomes, overseas, an accident waiting to happen—South Africa 2018 followed in the wheel ruts of India 2013, UAE 2014, England 2015, Sri Lanka 2016 and India 2017. The moral failure in Cape

Town was in the context of cricket failure: the desperate quest for a remedy to an all-too familiar predicament, the fielders straining to help the bowlers make good the failure of the batsmen, while hostile crowds, indifferent officiation and end-of-season fatigue contributed to an atmosphere of siege.

On 6 April, Cricket Australia went some way to acknowledging public dismay. Chairman David Peever foreshadowed two remedial processes, purifyingly "independent". A panel of past and present Australian players chaired by former Test batsman Rick McCosker and facilitated by Peter Collins of the Centre for Ethical Leadership would design a "charter that sets out standards of behaviour and expectations of Australian men's teams". This charter would be submitted to a wider review, supervised by Simon Longstaff of the Ethics Centre, into the "culture, processes and governance" of Cricket Australia, surveying the perspectives of stakeholders, including players and officials, by interview and questionnaire.

The 'cultural review' is a growingly familiar sporting phenomenon, as sporting bodies accustom themselves to being sizeable and diverse organisations where the quest for on-field success can lead to the toleration of aberrant behaviours. Such reviews can obscure as much as they reveal. Reviews at the West Coast Eagles and Essendon football clubs brought skeletons tumbling from cupboards; a 2017 review of workplace practices at the Australian

Olympic Commission by the Ethics Centre arranged the skeletons tastefully. In the meantime, CA has affected to move on, in advance of any prescriptions. There is a new captain, Tim Paine. There is a new coach, Justin Langer. There is a new chief operating officer, Kevin Roberts, widely perceived as CA's CEO in waiting. Longstaff was due to present his report in September. But there was no certainty it would be made public, in whole or part.

Yet there will remain a widespread sense that something is amiss—indeed, that as important as were the events of Cape Town, the ensuing public hue and cry was at least as instructive. Australian cricketers have always had their critics, and at times been easier to respect than to love. But they must seldom have felt so friendless as in the second half of their tour of South Africa. One saw, as one rarely does, the chinks of light between what are often casually elided—the Australian cricket team, Cricket Australia and cricket itself, the game and its place in Australian life.

Twice in the preceding four years there had been outbreaks of similarly intense feeling, spontaneously unifying in the death of Phillip Hughes in November 2014, lingeringly divisive in the industrial relations rumble between Cricket Australia and the Australian Cricketers' Association through 2017. Here was a third reminder, perhaps the most salutary of all, of cricket's uniqueness in the national imagination. The irony is that CA has in this decade ploughed prodigious energy into strategies that place "fans first", promising "a game for all". Yet they were oblivious to the disfavour into which the Australian team had slipped, despite market research that had apparently shown its "likeability" in decline. A commonplace sentiment after Cape Town was of cricket's votaries being "fed up", for which this brazen "cheating" was a final straw, rounding out a log of miscellaneous complaints, variously pointed, disgruntled and nostalgic. CA's intervention was couched in terms of the episode being an isolated ethical transgression; at least part of the public response saw events as the deepening of a general malaise.

That, I suspect, owes itself to Smith and Warner being the defining cricketers of their generation. Their successes have provided vindication for the 'system' that identified them young and progressed them rapidly: Smith had played ten Sheffield Shield matches when he first represented Australia; Warner had played none, and has still appeared in only 19, versus his 74 Tests. Their careers coinciding with the explosive growth of supranational T20 competitions around the world, they will likely retire as the wealthiest Australian cricketers of all time; by what transpired at Newlands, their reputations, and the game's, will also have been permanently marred. The same 'system' that has basked in their successes should not escape scrutiny amid their failings.

It was with this in mind that I decided to undertake my own 'cultural review'—less official and far cheaper, but genuinely independent. To this end I sought the views of 50 men and women in cricket whose opinions I respect: players, coaches, officials and observers past and present, including a dozen cricketers who have represented Australia in the last five years. I did so on a not-for-attribution basis; they responded with thoughtfulness and candour; often they were passionate; sometimes they were scathing. I will quote respondents anonymously here and there in these pages where they seem to have explained something pithily or pungently. But the opinions expressed, conclusions reached, and any errors are mine.

The reason for this is simple. Cricket Australia operates as monopoly and monopsony, unregulated, unrestricted and untaxed. If one wishes to work in the sport, there is every incentive to stay the right side of the country's sole promotor of cricket attractions and employer of cricket talent. Over the last decade, the organisation has also grown increasingly secretive and sensitive—paradoxically, with each year that it has grown richer and more powerful. Some who've raised questions these last few years have been penalised for their trouble. Asked to sum up the culture of Australian cricket, one of my interviewees put it more succinctly than I ever could: "Bullies and sycophants." Said another, by way of contrast: "[Australian rules] Football gives you one in the belly. Cricket gives you one in the back. It is full of good haters." Quoting them directly would hardly improve their employment prospects. But these voices do need a hearing. So, while the reviewers review, the administrators administer, the Australian team under Langer rebuilds, and Steve Smith, like Pinocchio, learns to be a normal boy, let us consider a beautiful game in a sometimes spiteful and vulgar age.

1

The End of Certainty

A key to understanding Australian cricket in the long run is grasping how decentralised it was for so long, how replete with checks and balances, sometimes to the point of inertia, but with a robust collective purpose.

The game was first organised by clubs, beginning about 200 years ago; from the middle of the nineteenth century, the most successful of these clubs began constituting associations to expedite intercolonial competition. At first these associations were starveling bodies. It was not officials but the leading players of New South Wales and Victoria who first formed the ambitions of visiting

England and of hosting inbound tours. It was one of the latter which, in 1892, resulted in the endowment of a fully-fledged first-class competition, the Sheffield Shield, which prospered, and the first national cricket body, the Australasian Cricket Council, which collapsed after seven years in the face of player distrust.

Not until 1905 were Cricket Australia's antecedent entities formed: the Australian Board of Control for International Cricket, to regulate the traffic of tours, and the Interstate Conference, to manage the Shield. These were not organisations so much as federations; they had no assets, no employees, no premises. They were instead regular meetings of delegates from the state associations, themselves delegates elected by first-grade clubs, with secretarial duties farmed out to one of the association secretaries, who performed them in addition to his usual duties. These meetings distributed the revenues raised by games and tours among the associations according to strict formulae, with which they kept the lights on and wheels turning. Strategies? Reserves? Barely. Agreeing on the day-to-day, over fixtures, selection, captains, committees, was hard enough.

To the outside world, Australian cricket presented a bold, bronzed and unified face; within, it knew considerable contention, which it diffused with little-changing devil-you-know arrangements. The board's voting and financial distribution structure barely changed in more than a hundred years; the apportionment of international fixtures followed a set pattern; the choice of teams precluded more than one selector from any state; likewise, when teams toured, captain, vice-captain and third selector had all to be from different states, the assumption being that two from anywhere would always gang up on their colleague.

The associations themselves were different. Some owned grounds and had to pay for their upkeep, others did not. Some served huge regional areas, others huge urban centres. For most of the 20th century, Tasmanian cricket was carved between three different bodies. There wasn't much flair; there was never terribly much money, and it never trickled down all that deeply; 'grassroots cricket', largely sustaining itself, was tended by volunteers. Parochialism posed problems: Western Australia and Tasmania were often treated like poor relations; New South Wales felt like a rich relative taken advantage of, and even contemplated secession in the early 1950s. Cricket's social conservatism was a hindrance: its administrators were drawn from a gene pool male and grey, inclined to take the public for granted, dismissive of player discontents about pay and conditions. And yet, and yet … the unifying forces—the passion for the game and the will to win, especially against England—remained stronger than the dividing ones. The preparation of players was Darwinian, the Shield a ruthless proving ground, and deciduous, personal and professional pressures curtailing most careers in their early 30s.

The Australian Cricket Board, as it became in 1973

by incorporating both Board of Control and Interstate Conference, began to change soon after, voluntarily and not. It obtained its first sponsor, the tobacco giant Benson & Hedges, which stayed the course for two decades; it agreed to terms with its first commercial broadcasters, having been inseparable from the ABC for four decades. One suitor, Kerry Packer's Nine Network, was so insistent that it engineered a shotgun wedding, with a dowry of exclusive rights. As an indirect result, the board became an incorporated entity. It was decided that the state association secretary responsible for board duties, David Richards from Victoria, should tackle them full-time as its 'executive director'. As the board's first full-time 'employee', and a Melburnian, he established the headquarters there, first at the back of the Victorian Cricket Association in Jolimont Street, then in an office building two doors away. The board became a public company in September 1982. Richards' responsibilities were circumscribed by the 'peace agreement' between the board and Nine, which for the first decade and a half of their relationship not only broadcast but marketed, merchandised and generally micromanaged cricket as well. Yet certain crucial steps were taken, not least the rollout of a modified game for children, Kanga Cricket, and a partnership with the Australian Institute of Sport in a new 'Cricket Academy' to incubate emerging talent.

On the accomplishments of that Academy's alumni, the teams led by Mark Taylor, Steve Waugh and Ricky

Ponting established a global cricket hegemony. The names come trippingly: Shane Warne, Glenn McGrath, Adam Gilchrist, Damien Martyn, Justin Langer, Brett Lee, Jason Gillespie, and the Michaels: Slater, Bevan, Hussey and Clarke. The same clannish and self-determining generation reinstated player influence in the game by forming a trade union, the Australian Cricketers' Association, in 1997: for the first time since the inception of the board, cricketers began partaking directly in the game's revenue, under the terms of a collective agreement called a memorandum of understanding. It was a bold step, but by relinquishing total control of cricket's finances, CA contained and mitigated many of the abiding tensions between players and administrators—a similar model of collective agreement and revenue sharing was subsequently adopted in New Zealand, South Africa and West Indies. Under CEO Malcolm Speed, what became Cricket Australia expanded its marketing, game development and communications capabilities, produced its first strategic plan under the durable rubric *From Backyard to Baggy Green*, and opened a new headquarters in Jolimont, again doors away.[1] Speed also hired a 33-year-old chartered accountant as general manager, commercial. Twenty years later, James Sutherland is still there.

Sutherland is tall, reserved and formal, seldom seen without a tie, and usually to be found in his office. When

---

1   The Australian Cricket Board/Cricket Australia have had three addresses on Jolimont Street, which faces on to the Melbourne Cricket Ground: 66 (1980), 70 (1980-2001) and 60 (2001-the present).

he posed with his greybeard directors as Speed's hand-picked successor in June 2001, he resembled a prefect mingling with a school's governors. Sutherland had played and coached cricket at first-class level while pursuing a commerce degree; he brought a similar discipline and dedication to his role. Social ease came less naturally. At work functions he would stand beside Michael Brown, CA's general manager, cricket, because Brown was a friendly cove who could converse with anyone; before public gatherings he would submit to careful coaching by Peter Young, CA's general manager, public affairs, always good-humoured and approachable. But he exerted quiet authority, including on reputational issues, endearing him to his board. An early challenge was in May 2003, when McGrath, following a string of such incidents, was involved in an ugly contretemps with the West Indian Ramnaresh Sarwan. Rather than merely invoke CA's code of conduct, Sutherland and Brown cajoled the members of Steve Waugh's team to draft and subscribe to their own behavioural manifesto, entitled 'The Spirit of Cricket'—a widely-praised initiative, and an example of Sutherland's process-oriented problem solving. As CA celebrated its centenary, its cricketers and their administration were benchmarks around the world.

Two forces ended that golden cycle, endogenous and exogenous. The former was natural attrition. In the 2006-7 Ashes, Waugh's successor Ponting led a team of the talents: Warne, McGrath, Gilchrist, Langer, Martyn,

Hussey, Clarke, Matthew Hayden and Andrew Symonds. In the 2009 Ashes, Ponting would lead, of these, only Hussey and Clarke. The volatility of results during that climacteric cost the number one Test ranking that Australia had enjoyed officially for more than six years and unofficially far longer. The structure around the team seemed in some respects meagre, merely forming part of Brown's outsized portfolio, with any needs funded from a small discretionary budget.

The other upheaval was financial: India's embrace of T20, and the world's. In March 2007, Australia completed an ODI World Cup threepeat without losing a match; India was despatched early, expensively, dismally. The next time Australia stepped on the cricket field, in September, it was beaten by Zimbabwe at Newlands, in its first game of the inaugural World T20, while India stormed to the title. Traditionally averse to the shortest format of the game, the Board of Control for Cricket in India experienced a Damascene illumination.

CA had a domestic T20 competition already: since 2005 the KFC-sponsored Big Bash had pitted the states, wearing their one-day uniforms, against each other, producing cricket of quality, drawing larger crowds than domestic 50-over games and gaining a promising following on Foxtel. The BCCI, modernising slowly from its licence raj origins, still did not: indeed, it had seen a businessman, Subash Chandra, roll out a private, made-for-TV version of T20, the Indian Cricket League.

Now it overtook its global peers in a bound. In July 2007, the BCCI invited CA and Cricket South Africa to a conclave where it shared plans hatched with the sports promotions and athlete management company IMG for a city-based T20 competition, the Indian Premier League; CA took advantage of the consultation to moot a related idea, a joint-venture annual tournament featuring the winners of each T20 domestic competition worldwide, the Champions League. They were launched together, rather like conjoined twins, even if one was clearly the appendage of the other. CA not only consented to its leading players featuring in the IPL but obediently discountenanced those who went to the ICL, including former internationals Michael Bevan, Jimmy Maher, Matthew Elliott, Michael Kasprowicz, Ian Harvey, Jason Gillespie, Ryan Campbell and Stuart Law.

The BCCI was a moody partner: in January 2008, it threatened to escalate Monkeygate at a cost in broadcasting and sponsorship monies to CA estimated at $60 million. India remained a challenging destination: in November 2008 the first Champions League had to be abandoned because of the attacks on Mumbai. Some at CA remained convinced that T20 was a fad. Even Sutherland at this stage was a sceptic. But the money was extraordinary. Sony paid $US1000 million to broadcast the IPL; rival ESPN, panicked by the sudden need for a T20 property, offered $US900 million for the Champions League; to acquire an individual IPL franchise, eight private capitalists forked out a total of $US724 million. Suddenly the Big Bash looked a little dowdy, and new options were white-boarded in collaboration with IMG, including a Southern Premier League involving teams from South Africa and New Zealand in the vein of rugby's Super 14, the rebranded southern hemisphere round-robin. But CA hastened slowly. Unlike Australian football, forced to modernise 25 years earlier by the collapse of its clubs' finances, cricket faced no immediate crisis: indeed, it had never been wealthier. As yet it saw its problems more narrowly.

The death of Pakistan coach Bob Woolmer cast a pall over the 2007 World Cup. Other careers were also rerouted. John Buchanan left the Australian coaching job on a winning note, Duncan Fletcher departed England on a losing note, and Greg Chappell ended with India on a sour note, concluding 20 months of worsening internal wrangles, even in the eyes of his hand-picked captain Rahul Dravid: "Tension is a good thing within a team, but it needs to be creative, not destructive." Chappell's trajectory since his retirement from playing ranks in 1984 has zig-zagged unpredictably. He was courted by the Liberal and National Parties in Queensland, dabbled in insurance and financial services, designed a coaching method called *The Chappell Way*, and published two books on health and fitness, while espousing the virtues of veganism. South Australia failed to win a trophy in his five seasons there; pitted politically against Sachin Tendulkar and Sourav Ganguly in India, his life expectancy in the sub-continent was never great.

In Australia, however, the Chappells will always be cricket royalty, albeit in contrast: Ian has kept the establishment at arms' length throughout his life; Greg has always been a welcome adornment; Ian has kept alive a spirited dislike of Sir Donald Bradman; Greg has mellowed from the days when players regarded Bradman as "the keystone of a grey wall of resistance" to improved financial rewards. In Greg's autobiography, in fact, he quotes with approval a conversation with Bradman in late life, who explained his resistance to professionalism as arising from a conviction that cricket was "a pastime". This resonated with Chappell on his return to Australia. He developed particular misgivings about the entente between CA and the Australian Cricketers' Association. Enhanced pay and conditions, he believed, had encouraged players to hang around first-class cricket, cluttering the system. He likened it to the county cricket he played with Somerset in the late 1960s, burdened by time servers and jobsworths; he diagnosed that Australia was now afflicted, similarly, by "the insidious nexus between professionalism and conservatism." And he accepted a job where, with his characteristic fixity of purpose, he could do something about it.

Since the winding up of the AIS Cricket Academy with

the sale of its Del Monte premises by the Australian Sports Commission, CA had been developing its own Cricket Centre of Excellence at a facility shared with Queensland Cricket at Allan Border Field, Albion. Sutherland saw it as a legacy project: a more ambitious facility than the Academy, consolidating coaching and sports science under one roof, in addition to accommodating young male and female cricketers at Griffith University. It had not, so far, been a raging success. Its management passed through several hands; its coaching ethos, biomechanically oriented, was criticised as being too theoretical; relations with the states, who had their own often quite different development programs, fluctuated; relations with the university were damaged by the antics of several young 'scholars', including a tyro David Warner, who was then suspended because of "repeated inappropriate treatment of accommodation facilities" at an apartment on the Brisbane River.

In May 2007 the Centre also lost its senior coach, Tim Nielsen, who succeeded Buchanan in the national role, and for the next year soldiered on in uneasy temporary hands. When CA management proposed as a successor Richard Pybus, the board decided that the successful English-born coach, then working in South Africa, was insufficiently prestigious; when the directors heard the name Greg Chappell, by contrast, they swooned. Here, it was felt, was just what the Centre needed: a guru, one with the same aura Rod Marsh had developed at the

Academy during his fruitful decade. Chappell enjoyed a well-founded reputation as a one-to-one batting coach. Still better, at a time Australian cricket faced change wrought by the eclipse of its great team, he came equipped with a persuasive long-term critique of the game in its current form.

For some years, Cricket Australia had been bandying about expressions like "high performance" and "pathway". They struck some as old wine in new bottles. Who wanted low performance? And weren't there pathways already? You got runs and took wickets for your club; then you got them for your state; then you were picked for Australia. It had been good enough for Bradman; good enough for the Chappells too; sure, there were under-19 competitions, even a national under-19 team, but the bolters of the Academy had still had to prove themselves in the Sheffield Shield before progressing to higher honours.

Chappell saw careers of the next generation having a different trajectory, young stars being plucked, incubated, challenged, and forced to adapt in order to advance. Of paramount importance was early identification. "Talent is like fruit," he would say. "If you don't pick it when it's ripe, it's likely to go off." Cricket's outstanding recent talents— Warne, Waugh, Ponting, McGrath, Brian Lara, Sachin Tendulkar—had all been blooded early at international level. The disappointments—Chappell spoke of "the Graeme Hick factor"—were those who had stagnated in first-class cricket, falling into bad habits. The exceptions—

players such as Adam Gilchrist and Mike Hussey, who had broken through later—he deemed mistakes, players who "probably should have been picked earlier."

The scheme had certain inherent appeals. Many careers lose direction between the ages of 19 and 23, as players progress from underage into open competition. First-class cricket was also increasingly compromised by the absence of top talent on international duties, leaving it hard to evaluate what runs and wickets were worth, and by the pursuit of parochial ends.

There existed obvious objections to the scheme too. It seemed calibrated to outliers. It did not allow for players maturing at different rates, even physically: expectations of a batsman, a fast bowler, a slow bowler and a wicketkeeper at age 23 have always differed. As a general point, early specialisation and junior excellence have not been found especially predictive of senior success in any sport—there is more support for the contrary point of view, that a sporting life of variety is far healthier. But to directors awed at the mention of his name, Chappell seemed to offer a strategy to develop "our next generation of champions"—and had not cricket in Australia favoured boldness? "Conservatism is not going to take us back to the top," Chappell urged in his autobiography. "We've always picked risk-takers who've changed the game, not followed it." The philosophy was influential on a board paper, *Australian Cricket Pathway Review*, presented by Michael Brown in March 2009, urging, inter alia, the appointment of a national talent manager. There was one outstanding candidate for that position and he relocated to Jolimont, from where he would network with talent managers in each state partly funded by CA.

Integral to Chappell's vision as national talent manager was an overhaul of cricket between first-grade and first-class level. There had been regular interstate Second XI and Colts competitions in Australia since around World War I, with some overlap. In recent years, however, Colts cricket had been supplanted by teams from the Academy and the Centre of Excellence, while Second XI cricket had matured into a strong competition in its own right. In 2008-9, the Cricket Australia Cup involved 14 fully fledged four-day round-robin games. It is remembered by participants as a stern initiation, young and old alike pitched into a scrap over rare spots in the Sheffield Shield. To Chappell, it was this rarity that was a problem. Australian cricket would hardly progress if it was recycling talent already tried and found wanting at first-class level—youth had to be given its head. So, in October 2009, CA announced a reconstitution of its Second XI competition as the Futures League, also including the Australian Capital Territory, with teams restricted to three players over the age of 23; matches were shortened to three days, for which spinners were compensated by there being no second new ball, and bonus points attached to their wickets.

Hindsight is always 20:20. And perhaps the conception of the Futures League has an outsized reputation as a strategic bungle, because it is seen as the thin end of the largeish wedge bending Australian cricket away from time-honoured principles of performance and merit and the gradual insinuation of well-meaning but too-clever-by-half artificialities. But in retrospect it has not stood up well. The 2008-9 Cricket Australia Cup featured more than a score of cricketers who would go on to represent Australia; among the top 20 scorers and wicket-takers in the 2009-10 Futures League, only three have earned baggy greens, and two had played the previous season. The net effect, it is now universally agreed, was a loss of talent: the Australian Cricketers' Association estimates as many as forty retirements among its membership in the four seasons age restrictions operated, concentrated among experienced grade cricketers whose Second XI opportunities had kept them in the game but who now saw themselves derogated as 'dead wood'. In hindsight, the consequences seem unambiguous: CA gained next to nothing from the experiment, and in the search for 'excellence' overlooked the contribution made by the very good, which after the wave of star retirements, and also the purdah of Australia's ICL signatories, it could ill afford. It would be a recurring mistake.

Ten years ago, of course, such esoterica as age restrictions in the Futures League rather eluded Australian cricket lovers, more concerned with how long Ricky Ponting and Mike Hussey would hang on, whether Michael Clarke and Simon Katich saw eye-to-eye, whether

Mitchell Johnson could bowl straight or Nathan Hauritz do otherwise. In fact, there was a sense of reassurance at having a past master such as Chappell at the controls of his own affirmative action campaign. As the board extended Tim Nielsen's coaching contract in August 2010, they also extended Chappell's remit by appointing him to Andrew Hilditch's selection panel, bumping long-serving Merv Hughes to make room—further, they made Chappell a second selection spokesperson, so that his proclamations about youth began reverberating like papal bulls. But hereabouts, despite Australia in the previous year having quietly stepped down to fourth in the ICC Test Championship table, CA's preoccupations also began wandering from the regeneration of the national team. There were other priorities, and these, it is true, were serious enough.

2

The Accountable Age

n mid-2010, Cricket Australia was grappling with two related challenges. The first was dealing with the promise and threat of T20. Two dozen Australians had just participated in a hugely-successful IPL 3; 34 were about to appear in Champions League 2, one of them, Mike Hussey, unwillingly. Hussey was desperate to play in a warm-up match on a short Australian tour of India; BCCI secretary Narayanaswami Srinivasan was just as keen that Hussey represent Chennai Super Kings, which he also owned, and Sutherland would override the player's objection. The notion of a Southern Premier League had now been overtaken by the concept of a fuel-injected

Big Bash, the Big Bash League, powered by intercity rather than interstate rivalries, new teams in new uniforms signifying a fresh start. CA's general manager, marketing, Mike McKenna envisioned a competition of eight franchise clubs, with two in each of the chief population centres of Melbourne and Sydney. To commence in 2012-13, it would dwell at first in the shadows of Foxtel, but eventually bask in the sunny free-to-air uplands, where the broadcast potential was heady. At some stage, indeed, it might relieve CA's dependence on revenues from India, and its vulnerability to the caprices of the BCCI.

The second challenge was updating a governance structure little changed for more than a century, so that it looked less like a federation, with a board composed of delegates, and more like a corporation, directors being chosen from whoever was best suited. There had often been talk of the duplication in Australian cricket, of CA and the state associations working at cross purposes, of the left hand not knowing what the right was doing; the associations were equally quick to push back at any hint of creeping centralisation. Initial response to the notion of introducing independent directors had persuaded Malcolm Speed that "you won't get the turkeys to vote for Christmas", and Sutherland's tentative speculations since that they might vote for Thanksgiving had not gone much further.

Even in 2010 there remained little appetite for reform on the board, particularly at the South Australian Cricket

Association, which with three votes out of 14, wielded by the formidable trio of CA's chairman Jack Clarke, former Labor premier John Bannon and former Howard government minister Ian McLachlan, enjoyed a sway out of all proportion to the state's demographics and its contribution to Australian playing ranks. There was also a lack of actual top-level playing experience on the board, for which directors tended to look to former captain Mark Taylor, steady and credible but only one voice. It was something of a risk for the executive to raise the subject again, but Sutherland had nimble minds at his disposal, including his new head of strategy, Andrew Jones.

Jones, a Stanford MBA, a former associate at McKinsey and a serious club cricketer with University of New South Wales CC, had first consulted to cricket on a 2004 strategic plan, and since provided similar services to associations of NSW, Victoria and Western Australia. He was disquieted by what he saw: a game with a public skewing old, male and white; an organisation, Telstra-like, unaware of the threat of competition. With general manager, game development Damien de Bohun and general counsel Dean Kino, Jones's input made the inaugural Australian Cricket Conference in September 2010, in the sylvan serenity of Aitken Hill Conference Centre, one of the most momentous gatherings in Cricket Australia's history.

Their approach was to tie the challenges of expansion and reform together by engendering an atmosphere of crisis and urgency. Cricket, Jones argued in a discussion paper, was losing popularity; cricket was old hat and white bread; cricket no longer reflected the tastes and priorities of the community, at least as these were delineated by market research. Already three-quarters of the way there, the BBL was yanked forward: plans for it were advanced by a year. "How well does Australian cricket work now?" was the Dorothy Dixer then posed at a panel discussion featuring Jones, Kino and other representatives of CA and state management. A chorus came forth: not well, or, at least, not as well as it should. It, and other working parties, amounted to an executive plea for a streamlined, independent board, and rather cornered the existing directors, especially the three South Australians.

A guest speaker, Boston Consulting Group's governance expert Colin Carter, then gave a presentation on the inception of the Australian Football League, of which he had been an important guiding hand, and a Commissioner from 1993 to 2006. As a Melbourne-based organisation, CA has always been subtly mesmerised by the winter code, once a co-habitant of Jolimont Street: Sutherland and his senior-most executives Brown and McKenna had all served long spells in Aussie rules, at Carlton, Hawthorn and Essendon respectively. The BBL, accenting cities rather than states, sought to emulate football's 'tribalism'. In September 2010 the AFL appeared unassailable: finals were then under way after a juggernaut season, with plans for teams on the Gold Coast and in Western Sydney shortly to fructify. Over the next few years, CA would object to the use of the phrase 'AFL-style Commission' to describe its newly fashioned board. But it was the example that directors had in mind when the day after Carter's talk they voted to seek from him a formal governance review. Carter would have for help another veteran of football's overhaul in non-executive director about town David Crawford, whose 1992 report to the AFL Commission led to its current structure. The turkeys had experienced a change of heart.

Christmas, meanwhile, also bore down on the directors' minds. As much as anything to do with appealing to a new generation, what had piqued interest in the BBL was money: specifically, the prospect of selling part or even the whole of the new franchise teams to external investors, as in the IPL. Blue sky billions were being bandied about. The irony is that CA's executive had gone cold on the idea of external equity in the BBL, believing the sums available were grossly overestimated and the implications of a dilution of control greatly underestimated: Jones warned wryly that there was "always free cheese in a mousetrap".

But CA would go through the motions of entertaining private ownership, partly to demonstrate why governance overhaul was necessary, because any such exercise would demonstrate the difficulty of reconciling the fiduciary responsibilities of directors serving on the boards of both CA and the state associations. Detailed external legal advice obtained in December 2010, in fact, was explicit:

"A common director may not, when sitting on the board of Cricket Australia, give precedence to the interests of his or her State Cricket Association over the interests of Cricket Australia, and the reverse is true also." It concluded that common directors seeking to act in the possible sale of interests in the new franchises "would find themselves in an impossible situation in seeking to discharge their duties to both companies." CA would retain Credit Suisse investment banker John Knox, a friend of Sutherland's, to run an investors' roadshow for the BBL in India; GMR, owner of the Delhi Daredevils, briefly had its foot on a minority stake in the Sydney Sixers. But the effort fizzled, having in the meantime done its work, illustrating how a part-time board of state delegates might be overtaxed by the issues before it.

Any short-term financial concerns were alleviated by other means. Jones, Kino, McKenna and chief financial officer Kate Banozic formed a working party offering options for a new financial model. After a decade's argy-bargy, CA had in 2000 agreed to divide their national income from broadcasting and sponsorship equally among the six states—a partial redress of the prior neglect of Western Australia and Tasmania. But this had left the four in five Australians located in NSW, Victoria and Queensland served by five in ten of Australian cricket's dollars. A year's back-and-forth ended with CA buying out the states' rights to host international cricket on a "no worse off" basis in which distributions were demarcated between core and strategic funding—a necessary precondition to the recommendations coming down the pike from Colin Carter and David Crawford. So, with the inaugural Australian Cricket Conference and the ensuing board meeting, CA came to a fork in the road and, as Yogi Berra once advised, took it. It also left a key detail out of account, visible in hindsight. In all the discussion of markets and models, directors and departments, the performance of the national team had not featured on the agenda. By the next agenda, it had surged to the top.

There have been inglorious seasons in Australian cricket, but as an *aestas horribilis*, 2010-11 stands alone, with its scoreline of three innings defeats by England. Worsening it all was the sense of haplessness, from the very start, when Australia led into the series with a mess of away Tests against India, home one-day internationals against Sri Lanka, and a ludicrous seventeen-member First Test squad forced to stand under umbrellas on a rainy day on Sydney's Circular Quay for—allegedly—promotional purposes. The board stood mute—in a sense already it was in caretaker mode. The executive had no choice but to act—or did it? In evaluating the Argus Review, from which so much in Australian cricket has proceeded, a good initial question is: was it even necessary?

The reasons for Australia's defeat were easy enough

to grasp. Playing stocks had weakened sharply: Stuart MacGill, Stuart Clark and Phil Jaques, who it had been hoped would palliate the losses of Shane Warne, Glenn McGrath and Matthew Hayden, had succumbed to chronic injuries; Andrew Symonds and Shaun Tait had been beset by mental demons; hopefuls like Mark Cosgrove and Dan Cullen had been waylaid by form and fitness challenges. As in 2005, England had an accomplished team peaking in unison; the team with which Australia concluded the series mustered fewer than 240 caps. When the inevitable injuries occurred, England amply covered the loss of a key bowler, Stuart Broad, while Australia was unable to replace its most reliable batsman, Simon Katich. Alastair Cook and Kevin Pietersen had the best summers of their careers; Ricky Ponting and Michael Clarke had the worst of theirs. What did this signify about the entirety of Australian cricket? Arguably less than was thought; the challenge was to its *amour propre*. Since Aitken Hill, CA had been in a mood of introspection. In addition to the inquiries commenced by Carter and Crawford, CA's executive was now mobilising for the Big Bash League, overhauling the financial model and mulling the medium-term outlook for a new strategic plan. Was there really scope for another review? Or was this also about the assimilation of a classic corporate ritual—the 'full report', the 'big picture analysis'?

A further preliminary question occurs: why choose a corporate chieftain to undertake this analysis? The review panel was composed of the preceding three Australian captains, Allan Border, Mark Taylor and Steve Waugh, and CA's previous CEO, Malcolm Speed, but the process was to be led by former National Bank boss and BHP Billiton chairman Don Argus. Argus is a storied Australian businessman, if not universally admired: by 2011, BHP's merger with South Africa's Billiton was seen to be an expensive fiasco. His preferred game had been hockey. He was a stranger to the inner workings of cricket—he had been a guest of CA at Test matches, but no more. There is an apocryphal story about Argus's appointment, that the businessman was said to have asked Sutherland: "So, James, what do you want in this review of yours?" It is too good to be true, of course, but it captures a sense, widely-held, that the review was designed to confirm conclusions already reached. Whatever the case, Argus's appointment, and also the tapping of the former management consultant Jones to operate the secretariat, carried an inference: that CA management saw the solution to Australian cricket's travails as ... further management. And perhaps that should not surprise us, for no management has ever seen the solution in less. To further polish the corporate veneer, Argus even brought in the consultants he had used for succession planning at BHP, American executive search firm Heidrick & Struggles, who surveyed "the cultural aspects of the team" with a questionnaire to contracted players containing such questions as, "Is your team a learning organisation?" and

"Are you tapping into people's discretionary effort?"

For the time being, let us accept that public alarm, Australia having slipped to an unflattering fifth on the Test rankings, demanded a visible response. The team's campaign to win a fourth consecutive World Cup was about to end at the quarter-final stage, closing Ponting's captaincy career. Coach Nielsen had lost confidence. National talent manager Chappell had not—which was an issue. The England and Wales Cricket Board (ECB) had undertaken a similar assaying process four years earlier, and seemed to have benefited by the Schofield Report, which had recommended a system of central contracts for core players and a shadow "performance squad". The Argus Review—more formally the Australian Team Performance Review—traversed the territory thoroughly, interviewing 61 people over two months. Most were obvious: the existing selectors, senior players and coaches. Others were less so: Olympic hockey coach Ric Charlesworth and AFL premiership coach Mick Malthouse. It was an early hint of cricket looking, quite reasonably, at trends in other sports.

Among both international and domestic players there was also strong support for the review. Although reasonably sanguine about the state of the game, they were strongly negative about the quality of coaching and selection, which had they felt had had a deleterious effect on the Australian dressing room. Surveys of the national team found that 47 per cent thought the coaching average or poor, and that "unpredictability of selection" had led to a "more selfish culture than we've seen in Australian cricket". A submission to Argus by the Australian Cricketers' Association argued that the "potential not performance" ethos associated with Greg Chappell had been counterproductive: "By gifting Australian selection to players before they have earned it, there is a genuine fear that we are not developing the hardened tough players we have in the past." Michael Brown had also stopped a few bullets too many: "There is a genuine lack of trust in the CA general manager cricket among the playing group … This is a significant impediment to a good relationship between CA and its players." There was satisfaction that change was in the air.

Yet misgivings formed early. What unsettled many was the presence of Sutherland during interviews—"ex officio and in a non-voting capacity", as it was explained—which hardly lent itself to a free and frank expression of ideas, with a current CA director (Taylor) and a former CA director (Border) on the panel already.

Argus thought in straight lines. Who was 'in charge' of the Australian cricket team? With the answer that it was complicated he was dissatisfied: he wanted something looking more like a bank, or at least a business. That determination to cut to the chase lent itself to senses of haste and of foreordination. "Mate we're running a bit behind," one interviewee recalls being told. "Might have to cut this a bit short." Having flown from interstate, he was in and out in ten minutes. "It was a total waste of time," recalls another well-qualified respondent. "They were basically answering their own questions." His interview left both impressions on captain Ricky Ponting, granted 30 minutes despite having "put on my best business suit", been "raring to go", and assuming his interview would "go on for hours."

In his brief appearance, Ponting did at least get a glimmer of where the review was headed. "So, Ricky," Argus began, "who do you think is accountable for the Australian cricket team's performance?" Ponting's answer of "the captain" was accepted with a satisfied nod. In the Argus Review's 40 pages, in fact, the words "accountable" or "accountability" would appear 43 times, and the phrase "high performance" 28 times, often in close proximity ("In high-performance organisations, measurement and accountability are a way of life and all leaders in the organisation must learn to link those measurements to high-performance outcomes"). At least, Ponting reflected later, he achieved one long-held ambition, even if it was too late for him to savour: the review would recommend that the Australian captain, and also the coach, become selectors, to "ensure appropriate authority and accountability".

Both, at stages in the 1980s, had. Misgivings had ended the practice. The Australian convention, at state as well as national level, had been that selectors should remain disinterested, and thereby objective. Captains had even preferred it that way. On the panel, Steve Waugh, in particular, had found the task trying on the 1997 and 2001 Ashes tours, while his decision to omit Shane Warne from a Test in Antigua in April 1999 had led to their permanent estrangement: "It was a big ask for, say, me and Gilly to tell a teammate he'd been dropped and that his income was consequently going to be cut by 75 per cent." Ponting did not see it that way. "Until the captain becomes a selector," he told Argus, "he can never be truly accountable for his team." Taylor and Border leaned with Waugh. Argus heeded Ponting, and also his likeliest successor Michael Clarke. "It's all about accountability," said Clarke when his turn came, again to Argus's satisfaction. So it was that Australian cricket took the advice of Argus, the former coach of Camberwell Hockey Club, over that of three distinguished Australian captains.

Two other selection changes were recommended, reversing decisions made two years earlier: one, that the role of chairman of selectors be full-time, effectively placing part-time chair Andrew Hilditch, and also his colleagues David Boon and Jamie Cox, on notice; two, that the national talent manager not be part of the panel, "to ensure greater focus in both areas". For Chappell's influence on Australian cricket, in fact, the review acted as a temporary curb. The Argus Review accepted part of his critique of Australian cricket—that, at 25, the number of CA contracted players was too many, at a cost, inevitably, to "accountability". Yet they also acknowledged "very strongly negative feedback" about the age-restricted Futures League, whose standards were perceived as poor, and whose knock-on effects on grade cricket had been felt, although the review panel lacked the courage of its convictions, agreeing to a slight relaxation of the age restrictions rather than insisting on its "preference" for a return to a fully fledged Second XI competition. The Futures League concept's fate was to be left, among many other things, to somebody else—a very important somebody else.

That figure was the most significant structural addition to the management flow-chart—in one way, the review's 'hero'. Following the example set by the ECB with the appointment of 'team director' Hugh Morris, which was actually following an example set by New Zealand Cricket, the Argus Review recommended the creation of "a single point of accountability within CA for Australian Team Performance", responsibilities carved out from Brown's existing role. The general manager, team performance, would stand athwart coach, captain, selectors, team manager, Centre of Excellence manager, state cricket managers et al in a system of "matrix management"—a structure connecting individuals with multiple lateral and longitudinal reporting lines, popularised by B-schools in the 1980s and widely used in banks. "He"—and the pronoun was assumed—would have responsibility for "people selection, development and performance management", "execution of agreed plans in coaching, team leadership, culture and selection", and "development and execution of the elite cricket pillar" of CA's next strategic plan.

Although it was vague about the attributes of this new majordomo, there was one hint at least about his base. The panellists heard "mixed views" about the "role and performance" of the Centre of Excellence—basically state coaches questioning its supervening influence on player management. But the edge that the Academy had given Australia on rival nations in the 1990s was fresh in the memory, and the Centre was a prestige project in which substantial sums had already been invested. In the CA vision, at the levels of governance and finance as well as talent management, national solutions were in favour, so the Centre enjoyed a timely reaffirmation, being "entitled to take responsibility for managing the development of current national team players and those who may play for the national team in future". Although it was not grasped at the time, that gave a Brisbane candidate for the new general managership a useful advantage in the recruitment process.

In retrospect, the Argus Review tends to be ridiculed: in the eyes of many I spoke to, it was variously "entirely useless" and "where the trouble started." Cooler appraisal detects more virtues. It upheld and reinforced core principles: a ten-round Sheffield Shield with a final to "support the production of long-form players"; the primacy of first-class and Test cricket, for which players "must be paid a premium". It is scattered, too, with thoughtful ideas, such as a "formal induction process" for new Australian players, and a clearer definition of the vice-captaincy and its relationship to the captaincy. It correctly foresaw some problems now widely diagnosed, and urged action that was not really taken, such as recognising grade cricket as "a vital part of the pathway system", taking steps to "retain outstanding players" in it, and an "active, accountable and specific approach to … succession planning" for players and administrators. And although it was not, strictly speaking, part of the review's remit, Jones recruited Argus to his scepticism of private ownership in the BBL: "Put simply, private owners will not have the same objectives as CA, so introducing them to the Australian cricket system risks compromising the achievement of CA's goals".

Like many a corporatist manifesto, however, it made heavy going of simple points, such as that elders should "lead by example" and "set a clear direction", that people should consult more and players should perform better. On the subject of "incentive systems", the review concluded: "These principles are standard in the corporate world and should be applied to Australian Cricket at the earliest opportunity". It neither explained why nor considered why not.

Nor can cricket help reading a little ludicrously when reduced to a fusillade of bullet points, jargon, abbreviations and arbitrary capitalisations: the coach and captain were responsible for "developing the team's vision and strategy", creating a "High Performance culture", embracing "Best practice transfer" and a "360-degree feedback process"; the chairman of selectors should be considered Australian cricket's "HR manager"; prospective cricketers would henceforward be "PONIs", or "Players of National Interest". And the point it hammered away at, about "accountability", was ultimately redundant: few games are judged less sparingly than cricket, with its bare accounting of every individual performance, and the harsh light of their interpretation.

As the Argus Review proceeded, of course, the show had to go on; likewise the toll of anno domini. When Australia lost to India in the quarter-finals of the 2011 World Cup, Ponting handed back his captain's commission, clearing the way for the long-awaited succession of vice-captain Michael Clarke. The appointment was not universally popular. For all his playing skill and tactical acuity, Clarke had all the narrowness and self-involvement of one who left school at 16 to play cricket, had an agent when he was 18, and an Australian cap at 21. The ambitious deputy in a faltering team, too, is a conflicted figure, favoured by the combination of individual success and collective failure. In the three years he had been number two, Clarke had enjoyed the office without dwelling on the responsibilities, although Ponting loyally endorsed his promotion. Clarke also often seemed to have more friends outside the team than in—one of them, for a gossipy period, an accident-prone celebrity fiancée, Lara Bingle. Yet cricket teams take all sorts and are used to contingent friendships and temporary alliances. Ponting having smoothed Clarke's path, Taylor flattened it at board level.

Less thought was given to the choice of Clarke's deputy. At the time, it could be argued that Shane Watson was Australia's most valuable player, near enough to a first pick in all three formats. Over 18 months, he had turned an ersatz opening partnership with Simon Katich into the most effective in the world; his medium-pace variations were reliable and accurate. He was a meticulous, sensitive cricketer with a body like a Formula One racing car, possessed of huge power but prone to mishap. He had been close to Ponting, and thrived on his confidence; he was altogether less enamoured of Clarke, and the feeling was mutual. "He'll always let you down," the captain would mutter of his deputy's fitness record—hardly in compliance with Argus's recommendation that "the captain should … actively seek and use the counsel of his vice-captain, which is an important role and should be more clearly defined".

In fact, Clarke had no interest in sharing responsibility. He instantly saw the team as his. On a brief one-day international tour of Bangladesh, the new firm made a successful start, Clarke stroking an assured 101 in the first game, Watson a barnstorming 185 not out in the second, Hussey a crisp 108 in the third.

Another transition was also handled, and another link to the past severed: Australia's long-serving team manager Steve Bernard handed over responsibilities to Gavin Dovey, a former team operations manager with the Rugby Football Union, recommended to CA by the ECB's Hugh Morris. But while CA awaited the deliberations of the Argus Review, the sky was scanned for omens, and one was detected in June. When the contract list was unveiled, no room could be found among the 25 names for Katich, despite his averaging 50 in Test matches over the preceding three years.

Katich was 35 years old—relevant insofar as so were Ponting and Hussey. Hilditch's panel was making use of its time ahead of the Argus Review's presentation by making changes with a free hand, new fancies including Shaun Marsh, Usman Khawaja and Trent Copeland. With a top six filled out by Clarke and Watson, the selectors argued, that left no scope for another older batsman. It was a curious long-term call by a panel with a short-term future—defiant even. And it was vigorously debated, including by the forthright Katich, who in a memorable press conference at the SCG tipped a baggy green bucket on the selectors and the system, in which there were "rules for some and rules for others" that he "was not going to lie about". To prove a cussed point he would play a further 35 first-class matches, averaging 50. A common hearsay interpretation was that Katich had fallen foul of Clarke, with whom he had had a well-known dressing room confrontation in 2009. It was surmise, and almost certainly erroneous: Clarke bore no responsibility for the contract list, formal or informal. But it contained a timely warning of the risks inherent in a captain serving on a selection panel—a warning too late for the Argus Review to heed.

C larke's team was in Sri Lanka a month later when Don Argus's handiwork was finally tabled, and caused, as it were, an immediate 'spill' of positions. Coach Nielsen, reduced to tears, suddenly faced the prospect of reapplying for his post, which he elected not to do; Sutherland's right-hand man Michael Brown, who had found his job split in half, was also not long for the organisation. The selectors signed off with a final few off-the-wall picks, one standing up very well in hindsight: the teenage speedster Patrick Cummins was picked for a debut tour of South Africa. The players made plain their disenchantment with Chappell all the same, shunning him at dinner on tour, and excluding him from the dressing room.

The more important vacancies resulting from the Argus Review were new, the first filled after a two-month search. Cricket Australia's new general manager, team performance, would be neither of cricket nor only Australia. Thirty-seven-year-old Pat Howard had earned his coaching spurs at the Leicester Tigers after playing 20 Tests for the Wallabies and before managing a new high-performance unit at Australian Rugby Union. Organised, energetic, gregarious and numerate, he held a couple of advantages over rival applicants such as Tom Moody and Dean Jones: he was based in Brisbane, near the Centre of Excellence, and had project management experience as the chief financial officer of Cromwell Property Group, bound to be handy in the centre's further evolution. His disadvantages, meanwhile, were just about everything else: his knowledge of cricket was negligible, although in a certain light this could be seen as a freedom from the encumbrances of tradition, superstition and the old boys' network. He was the choice of an organisation keen to embrace new approaches, new learnings. Dean Jones was not even granted an interview.

The choice of coach, involving Howard alongside Sutherland, Mark Taylor and John Allen from Crank Sports, was also that of a system questing beyond itself. Mickey Arthur had evolved from a battling first-class cricketer to a successful national coach in South Africa before stumbling in the briar patch of the country's racial preoccupations. Moving to Perth, where the Proteas had won a remarkable Test match in December 2008 on the way to a memorable series victory, Arthur had coached Western Australia for a year, and cast his hat into the ring almost on a whim.

Everyone liked the avuncular, unassuming Arthur, comfortable in backgrounds, averse to confrontation. There were solid internal candidates, already part of

Nielsen's backroom, including batting coach Justin Langer and fielding coach Steve Rixon. Again, though, the climate favoured change and challenge, with Howard having previously recruited the New Zealander Robbie Deans to coach the Wallabies—the first foreigner to do so. Coincidentally, even as CA searched for its new coach, Deans's tenure was beginning to sour, with a limp World Cup campaign in New Zealand. But Arthur was nudging at an open door, laid with a welcome mat: where selection in South Africa had been about politics as much as personnel, here, thanks to Argus, Arthur would be a selector alongside his captain. He joked about missing his home country's chaos: "Here I just talk to Pat, something happens, and it's done. Amazing."

Between times, CA named the coach's selection colleagues, the hardy West Australian pair of Rod Marsh and John Inverarity, the latter interviewing successfully for the role of chairman (or National Selector, in the new nomenclature). There was a hint here of traditional thinking, as a counterbalance to the newbies—they were old confederates of CA's incoming chairman Wally Edwards, having set in motion the decades in which Western Australia won the Sheffield Shield more often than not. As it was, they were in an awkward situation. As captains of WA, they had had no formal selection role, and considered this arms-length relationship preferable. Now they found themselves on a panel featuring captain and coach, who often as not voted en bloc. Arthur regarded part of his role as being to 'support' Clarke come what may, much as he had the Proteas' Graeme Smith; Clarke liked being supported. The skipper, fortunately, was also entering a deluxe career phase, a 30-innings sequence in which his Test average swelled from 46 to 53, while Ponting, Hussey and the rugged keeper-batsman Brad Haddin buttressed the middle order.

Further complications existed: the reconfiguration of the Sheffield Shield to accommodate the new Big Bash League left the selectors with no first-class form to refer to after early December, even as the summer's Test matches ran to the end of January; the stop-start nature of competition made fitness and match readiness difficult to evaluate, especially for pace bowlers, but also for batsmen. For Boxing Day 2011, for example, Australia recalled from injury Shaun Marsh, who had played a single BBL innings in seven weeks, and who not surprisingly eked out 17 runs from six hits in three Tests against India. Yet this was the reality of a game now enjoined to 'put fans first'.

3

Ashes Battle, Talent War

A digression: 'fan', dictionaries tell us, is an Americanism, originated in the 1880s in the context of baseball, with a mildly pejorative connotation. The baseball 'fanatic', of which fan was a shortening, was first of all a bore with a head full of facts. Before World War II, 'cricket fan' was used in Australia far less often than the expression 'cricket lover', who was, of course, chaste and courtly. The spread of 'fan' here perhaps manifested the influence of 'Austerica'— architect Robin Boyd's word for Australia's wholesale cultural borrowing from the US from the 1950s. 'Fan' still does not have the field to itself in England, even in its biggest sport: Premier League followers remain 'football supporters'. But here it is all-purpose, in keeping with sport's tendency to hyperbole and its air of safety, for in other contexts fanaticism is a scary notion. The 'cricket lover' is now the buffer, the duffer, the rheumy-eyed romantic.

The 'fans first' concept should be credited to the sharp-minded strategist Andrew Jones, who presented it as the first of four 'pillars' in CA's updated strategic plan, adopted by the board in October 2011. The key to any successful business, Jones said, was a focus on the customer—a constituency that cricket, he argued with some force, had tended to take for granted, or at least treated as uniform.

The Big Bash League, for which he was an articulate advocate, represented a tilt at a new audience, in addition to diversifying CA's income and making more intensive use of cricket's infrastructure. Seeking to build an urgency around this encouraged a certain radicalism: this 'fan' went from seemingly nowhere to the top of CA's priorities. Even cricket suffered a kind of demotion in BBL, part of, rather than central to, the colourful, noisy spectacle for the sake of the spectator developing a vague association of the game with a generalised feeling of good times as corporate messages flashed past. When the Scorchers hosted the Sixers for a game played in gear inspired by Batman and Superman, the action was barely distinguishable from the advertisements. Dan Migala, the American consultant who helped CA frame the BBL as a "family night out", put it succinctly: "One of the mantras we have worked on with the BBL is to . . . deliver entertainment that also happens to have a cricket match involved."

'Mantra' is another flavoursome word, literally an utterance that by constant repetition induces an altered state. And if the BBL did not quite transfix Jolimont, it certainly drew other parts of the game towards it, not least at junior level, where the Milo T20 Blast became the bite-sized morsel of cricket easiest to sell to enthusiastic children and time-poor parents, and where white ball cricket become the predominant form in under age carnivals.

Arguments about the merits of the BBL in particular and T20 more generally are long moot. It should be allowed that there are plenty of dull Tests and pointless one-day internationals; also, that the benefit of bad T20 is that at least it is over quickly. At the same time, there are entailments. It is far from obvious that T20 operates, as it is claimed, as an invitation to other forms of cricket, as distinct from being merely a gateway to more of itself. It is potentially worrying that the quality of T20 tends to be regarded as of such little moment providing a standardised entertainment product has been delivered; this arguably does not exalt the fan at all, rather it treats them as just a bit stupid. Nor, at least in the short term, did the putting of 'fans first' always reconcile so easily with another pillar of CA's strategy: that of producing "the best players, teams and officials".

W hat of those officials? In January 2012, Colin Carter and David Crawford presented *A Good Governance Structure* for Australian Cricket to CA's new chairman Wally Edwards. Rejecting arguments for the federal structure in terms of the "uniqueness of cricket", they proposed that the existing 14 delegates give way to a maximum of nine non-executive directors, none of whom could hold office simultaneously in any state administration, seeing such a move as a necessary step toward modernisation.

Edwards is an engineer by background and entrepreneur by inclination, the owner of the irrigation supply company Holman Industries; he is affable, shrewd, a sniffer of breezes. Back in the day, he had been an old-fashioned apologist for state rights, remembering his first board meeting in 1996 for the advice of hard-bitten colleague Barry Shepherd: if many things in life were uncertain, one thing you could rely on was that "the Vics are pricks". Since Aitken Hill he had changed his tune, in light of what he could see was a changing game.

Carter and Crawford responded to one fear expressed by the old guard, that an independent board would simply consolidate power on the eastern seaboard: their plan required that at least one director reside in each state.

That still failed to satisfy South Australia, but Kino designed a two-stage voting process to circumvent their resistance while Edwards carefully talked around the other state associations with a timetable that was an exercise in gradualism.

A revised constitution recognised the associations as CA's shareholders with three votes each, and an interim period allowed Edwards, Victorian Earl Eddings, Tasmanian Tony Harrison and, at last, Bannon to continue by standing down from responsibilities at their associations. A nominations committee—composed of Argus, veteran insolvency practitioner Tony Hodgson and two state chairmen—then chose from a suite of candidates paraded by Neil Waters of the recruitment agency Egon Zehnder. If the old board had sometimes looked a little like a car geared to reverse into the future, the new was a push-me-pull-you, not quite fully representative, not quite completely independent, arguably reflecting less the present than CA's blazered past and its big-end-of-town ambitions, with Jacqui Hey and David Peever bringing experience from Qantas and Rio Tinto respectively. Kevin Roberts, a former executive at adidas, at least had 23 first-class games for New South Wales on his CV. The return of Mark Taylor, initially excluded, was a useful enhancement, providing what might otherwise have been thin cricket credentials.

The only recommendation of *A Good Governance Structure* that went unapproved was for the promotion of the CEO to a fully-fledged executive director with a vote, as was the case in the AFL. But in other respects, with the admiring Edwards continuing as chairman, Sutherland's authority was consolidated, and reinforced by an executive makeover, following the departure of Michael Brown to run soccer's Asia Cup. A new tier of management was created featuring five executive general managers: Howard, team performance; De Bohun, game development; McKenna, operations; Kate Banozic, finance; and two new recruits. Marianne Roux, former head of talent at human resources consultancy Mercer, took on the portfolio of 'people and culture'; Ben Amarfio, previously general manager of the radio network Austereo after managing broadcasting and digital activities at the AFL, came to run media, communications and marketing. Remuneration was increasingly geared toward bonuses based on surpluses—an understanding of cricket's growing financial needs, if an odd eventuality in a not-for-profit organisation.

Further changes followed. The likeable De Bohun left to become head of the A-League, to be succeeded by another well-credentialled corporate pick, Orica executive and Harvard graduate Andrew Ingleton. The public observed the constantly changing faces beneath the baggy greens wondering what it all meant; but at Jolimont, the turnover was at least as great, and perhaps more meaningful.

Nobody shook the scene to the degree of Pat Howard.

In his first summer in charge, Howard manifested the qualities by which he would become known. He was busy—always busy. He was direct—sometimes to a fault. He was impatient with cricket's oral traditions; he liked players sorted into rankings, concepts expressed as numbers. Who were Australia's 25 best pace bowlers in numerical order? What was a Test average at which a batsman was dropped? What was the first-class average at which a batsman earned promotion? He seemed to know Don Argus's conclusions to the last bullet point, to the extent that Edwards would joke: "Pat, the Argus Review isn't our bible. It's a guide." He saw a game reliant on folk wisdom, full of archaisms and superstitions, which he wished to replace with rigour and data. Not surprisingly, his benchmark was the All Blacks, to whose success a system of Individual Player Profiles seemed fundamental. Howard drew their high-performance director Don Tricker and player development manager Mike Anthony to Australia, where they presented to a conference at the Australian Institute of Sport, and acquired the relevant intellectual property as the basis of a new Athlete Management System. How many balls you bowled or hit today; how well you slept last night; your latest skinfold; your last 2km time trial: Howard wanted to know it all. International teams began conversing in their own WhatsApp chat groups. Being added to that chat group upon selection became almost as much an initiation as receiving one's baggy green, and at least one got to keep the latter: deletion from the group after omission was like a drumming from the corps.

Just as cricket had been slow to reckon with technology, Howard said, it had been loath to acknowledge the cut-throat competition with rival sports for youthful flesh. In April 2010, cricket had taken visible pride in wresting teenage all-rounder Alex Keath from AFL football's maw, to the extent of rewarding him with the job of 13th man in a Test match. But Keath was just one among many. The challenge was to build "the biggest talent pool" in Australian sport, where the "best talent" was "choosing cricket"—the chief task lay in the elite game's limited dimensions. Ever the numbers man, Howard pointed to there being just the six state squads. Only 66 players, therefore, could appear in any single Sheffield Shield round, compared to close to 400 players in an AFL round, more than 200 in an NRL round, and even more than 150 in an A-League round.

In a presentation entitled *The War for Talent*, he laid out a plan to significantly expand cricket at under-15 and under-17 level and to accelerate its progress with a "CA junior rookie pool" of about 100 teens chosen from a draft camp and allocated to state or regional centres, with states given incentives to "bring on two rookie contracts per year". Howard wanted to force earlier "talent decisions", to cement their players' "passion and relationship with the game". There was talk for the first time of a "national performance squad" at the Centre of Excellence, which would become the basis of an additional team composed of rookies in the one-day Matador Cup.

The War for Talent shared a title and ideas with popular 2001 management textbook by three consultants from McKinsey, which argued that the success stories of the modern economy shared the "deep-seated belief that having better talent at all levels is how you outperform your competitors". Who had the most stars won—a superficially attractive notion given that stars in all fields are those we are taught to admire. In fact, the infatuation with individual brilliance was also discovered to be an obstacle to collaboration and a precondition of destructive hubris—Malcolm Gladwell's 2002 *New Yorker* essay, 'The Talent Myth', is a famous debunking. By the time Howard borrowed it, almost half the companies cited by the McKinsey authors had either disappeared, lost huge sums of money, or in the case of the most celebrated example of a talent warrior, Enron, both. But as often happens in management theory, the "war for talent" lingered as a zombie idea, and in a sport setting had an appealing ring.

Many detected the influence of Greg Chappell, with the plan's idea that champions proclaim themselves early; its in-your-face question was: "If you can't make State team and NPS team and you are over a certain age, should you be in the system?" Some heard AFL-speak in objectives such as to "create list churn": was it quite cricket, as it were, to harvest elite athletes simply in order to flip them in search of stars? The plan went back for revision—the concept of a draft camp, for example, never found support. But in cricket the "war for talent" became a kind of philosopher's stone, having also a personal dimension for James Sutherland: his multi-talented son Will, who turned 13 in October 2012, already looked like facing a Keath-style decision. As pathways competitions continued their expansion in ostensible parallel to the existing grade and premier cricket competitions, there was even a commercial imperative. With eight Big Bash League franchises, cricket would need more warm bodies, especially given the on-going unavailability of senior players on international duty.

In the meantime, ever a glutton for complex tasks, Howard took on another, acting as CA's representative in the negotiation of the next collective agreement with the Australian Cricketers' Association. The ACA's chief executive, Paul Marsh, was bemused: how could Howard work alongside the players—as effectively a colleague—then across the table from the players' duly appointed industrial representatives? Marsh strove to deal as much as possible with Sutherland, and to leave the legal minutiae to his colleague Mike Abrahams and CA's Kino. Still, the message from Jolimont was clear. As recommended by Argus, CA wanted to hand out fewer contracts, and wished pay to track performance more closely.

There was a paradox to this. Wouldn't the objective of ranking number one in all three formats require greater degrees of specialisation and therefore more players rather than fewer? But the ACA decided to fall in with the new dispensation: Marsh was broadly supportive of CA recommitting to international cricket in line with the thrust of the Argus Review. The new memorandum of understanding would be longer, five years, narrower, with a core group of 17 contracted players, and more complex, with a formulae based on wins and ICC rankings, than any previous deal. Instead of the old 26 per cent share of Australian Cricket Revenue—total revenue less agreed carve-outs—the players would start the contract period on a base level of 24.5 per cent with the potential for this to increase to 27 per cent.

To players, it still sounded a little odd. Would a few "at risk" dollars make a Hussey try harder? A Brad Haddin? A Peter Siddle? Addressing Australia and Australia A squads gathered in Darwin for a winter training camp in August 2012, Sutherland was challenged about his proclamations that players were no longer being "paid to play" but "paid to win". Ponting, a conscience if no longer captain, is recalled as responding sceptically: "Hang on. We get 'paid to win'? We get paid to play the best we possibly can. And yes, a lot of the time that will mean we win. But that will not mean we win all the time. So that means we don't get paid?" There was no turning back. Arthur's piping voice was heard wafting over the training session: "Remember! You're not being paid to play! You're being paid to win!" As was he: his $400,000 package stood to be sweetened by half as much again in bonuses.

Not long after, a disenchanted Langer swapped his post as Australia's batting coach for the task of coaching Western Australia, roping in his old mucker Katich to captain the Perth Scorchers in the BBL—the beginnings of a remarkable ascendancy for both.

More ups and downs awaited Australia's new regime. India and Sri Lanka were convincingly disposed of at home, West Indies away. Australia has hardly played better T20 cricket than in 2012's World T20, stumbling only in the semi-final. Promising beginnings were made by Mitchell Starc and James Pattinson in Test cricket, George Bailey and Clint McKay in one-day cricket. Though deprived by injury for much of the time of vice-captain Watson and strike bowler Mitchell Johnson, Clarke's team would have won back their number one Test ranking had they winkled out the last two South African wickets at the Adelaide Oval in December 2012.

Clarke himself grew in stature, if never quite in vernacular appeal, a captain wonderfully intuitive on the field, indefinably conspiratorial off it, his communion with Shane Warne a curious affair that probably worked for them both, lending Clarke stature and Warne relevance. Clarke certainly appealed to *The Australian* newspaper: in 2012, it anointed him Australian of the Year; in 2013, it concluded he was the most powerful man in Australian sport, by dint of his captaincy, skill as a batsman, responsibility as a selector and recognisability as a figure; in contrast to the insouciant Ponting, Clarke cared deeply about such perceptions. He set his life as he set his fields, fastidiously. When Howard, Inverarity and Marsh presented to the new CA board on the Australian team's progress in February 2013, the directors gave the Clarke/ Arthur ticket unqualified endorsement. But summer ended on an autumnal note, with the retirements in short order of Ponting and Hussey, proud cricketers curiously out of step with the new order. In their absence, the team, after its tentative step forward, took two back.

Chandigarh's JW Marriott Hotel is a glassy five-star at the great planned city's busiest roundabout, Piccadilly Chowk. The Australian cricket team that stayed there in 2013 after losing the first two Tests seemed likewise to be going in circles. At 7pm on 10 March, there was a meeting of the squad's management: under discussion was the training for the two days before the Third Test in Mohali; also unfinished business from the Second Test in Hyderabad, after which each team member had been asked to present, in some medium, even if only by text, three areas for potential improvement. As is now remembered, there were four defaulters: Watson, Johnson, Khawaja, Pattinson. Carefully teased out in Daniel Brettig's *Whitewash to Whitewash*, the subsequent events require little reiteration.

No beaten team is happy, but this one was unusually at odds. As an experienced administrator put it to me:

"You have 25 people sitting in a hotel for a week with a step being contemplated like this, and nobody says to anybody else: 'You'd better do your homework.' How does that happen?" It happens when captain and vice-captain are obviously estranged; at the time, Clarke saw no point picking Watson while the latter was prevented from bowling by a calf injury; Watson sensed it; Johnson sympathised. Then as Johnson himself wrote: "Usi and Patto got caught in the crossfire."

As a snapshot of a culture more broadly, Homeworkgate could be considered the Sandpapergate of its time. Both involved lines of player behaviour—attempts to define one in 2013, failure to live one in 2018. There are differences too, of course. In 2013, players had failed to perform a team duty; in 2018, they transgressed a law of the game. But both, to put it crudely, dramatise the difficulties of coaches earning thousands a year exerting discipline on athletes earning millions a year, and involve important meetings making spur-of-the-moment resolutions with better intentions than foresight.

Consider, first of all, the composition of the group around Clarke: Arthur's coaching staff of Steve Rixon, Michael Di Venuto, Ali de Winter and Dene Hills, the medical team of Alex Kountouris, David Bailey, Grant Baldwin, Dr Peter Brukner and Dr Michael Lloyd, team manager Gavin Dovey, security man Frank Dimasi, public affairs manager Matt Cenin and website cameraman Adam Goldfinch. The size disguised a relative lack of experience. The last of Rixon's 13 Test caps had been earned 29 years earlier; since Langer and McDermott had moved on, nobody else had any. With the duty selectors swapping, Inverarity flying home as Marsh was flying in, there was little grey hair around either. The strongest voices in the discussion, according to Brettig's account, were those with the least cricket background: Dovey, from rugby, on a first tour of India; Brukner, from Australian football and soccer, on a first tour. They had been irked by an undertone of laxity and sloppiness on tour, albeit that these were arguably symptoms rather than causes. With Arthur, whose vocabulary of profanity extends no further than 'sherbet', Brukner's words struck home: "They think you're not tough enough, Mickey." Then, so did Clarke's: "Whatever you decide, I'll support."

Here may be the least explicable aspect of Homeworkgate: that Clarke, whose captaincy was born into the era of "accountability", who relished and craved and crusaded for it, in the end affected to place himself behind his reluctant coach, "swayed by the strength of feeling among the support staff"—hardly what Don Argus had in mind when he asked who was in charge of the Australian XI, and whom he also insisted be "the principal spokesman for the team". When the decision was announced, in fact, Clarke even tried to distance himself from it, refusing at first to answer media questions until Sutherland insisted. When Clarke did, five years before Sandpapergate made it common coinage, the C-word got a mention: "If you play for Australia, there is a lot that comes with that, and standards, discipline, culture are all a big part of what we're talking about." But a culture necessitating such crudity of discipline is a failure. Nor was the matter helped by Pat Howard's needless but widely-reported aspersion on Watson: "I know Shane reasonably well. I think he acts in the best interests of the team sometimes."

The twists of fate kept coming: Watson captained Australia in the Fourth Test at Delhi in the absence of the injured Clarke; Watson then lost the vice-captaincy to Clarke's close compadre Haddin, who in India had not even been the first-choice 'keeper; Clarke, more or less willingly, relinquished his selection responsibilities, at the urgings of Rod Marsh, and also Allan Border, acknowledging their burden; the CA board expressed full confidence in Arthur.

The last of these, as for many a football coach, proved instantly perishable.

A short walk from Birmingham's Hyatt Regency, the Walkabout Inn was a convenient spot for disappointed Australians to mingle with successful English rivals after their day's Champions Trophy match on 8 June 2013, which perhaps encouraged a longer than usual stay. David Warner's woozy swing at Joe Root at 2am ended up knocking out his coach. Three days after Warner's suspension, Arthur paid with his job.

With less than a fortnight to the commencement of a unique back-to-back Ashes cycle—a ten-match, two-hemisphere broadcasting bonanza—a replacement was needed in a hurry. The most obvious candidate had filled in previously and was on hand: Troy Cooley, head coach at the Centre of Excellence, was in England with Australia A, on a two-week tour to conclude in Bristol ahead of the Test matches. But Sutherland and Howard looked past Cooley to his batting assistant, Darren Lehmann, in his first CA role in the five years since he had completed an expedited Level 3 coaching course at the Centre of Excellence, six months after ending a two-decade first-class career.

Three years earlier, Lehmann had been deemed a little raw and rough to coach Australia's under-19 team. Suddenly, the national team seemed in need of a happier tone and hornier hands. Sutherland had known the leathery 43-year-old Lehmann more than twenty years. Howard and Rod Marsh had been studying Australian coaching ranks some time, observing the lack of former senior players, disappointed that the likes of Glenn McGrath and Jason Gillespie had ended up abroad. Lehmann himself had had to obtain his start in the Indian Premier League before helping Queensland win two domestic trophies. Howard viewed such appointments as adding credibility to a system of "coaching pathways" he had in mind.

Now, Lehmann was on hand, if not perhaps ready.

When Howard asked him over lunch about coaching Australia, Lehmann thought he was talking about in some unspecified future; in fact, Howard saw the future starting the next day. Easing into his first press conference, Lehmann laid claim to an 'Australian way' of cricket that had always eluded the South African Arthur: "The team is going to play a certain way, an aggressive brand of cricket that entertains people and fans but also gets the job done on and off the field."

On the plus side, the brevity of Lehmann's preparatory time prolonged his honeymoon period. Little store was set by what the team might accomplish in the five Tests in England; it was simply hoped that Australia would do enough to narrow the gap before the five Tests in Australia. Nobody expected instant miracles. In fact, Michael Clarke's team surpassed all expectations. Within a year, they had recaptured the number one Test status for the first time in nearly five years. Nine months after being bowled out for 128 on a flat second day wicket at Lord's, Australia marmalised a first-rate South African team including Hashim Amla, AB De Villiers, Dale Steyn and Vernon Philander at Newlands by 245 runs. Yet, considering the resurgence demonstrates the difficulty in cricket of separating cause from effect. For the cycle of 2013-14, Australia had already put faith back in experience. In addition to Haddin, Inverarity's panel recalled the hard-working opener Chris Rogers (35) and the hard-charging seamer Ryan Harris (33); Watson, too, was restored to fitness, greatly enhancing the team's balance. Though Mitchell Starc bowled through pain into incapacity in the one-day series in England, that made space for the enigmatic Mitchell Johnson. Johnson had always bowled like lightning, including never twice in the same place; for a period of six months, he was a perfect storm of pace and precision, taking 59 wickets at 15.23 versus 254 wickets at 31.46 in the rest of his career.

This leaves questions to consider. Was the decisive coach here Lehmann, whom CA lauded itself for appointing, or Dennis Lillee, whom CA declined to pay a success fee despite Johnson crediting him with single-handedly rebuilding his action and confidence? Was the 5-0 home Ashes scoreline a dividend of the high-performance investment of the years since the Argus Review, or a last extraction from the reserves laid down in the preceding golden generation? Rogers, Australia's highest scorer across the ten Tests, had very nearly been axed by Victoria the year before his comeback, felt to be too old and too limited despite churning out industrial quantities of first-class runs—it had taken Inverarity's personal intervention to rescue him from a twilight in county cricket.

Ah, who cared? Here was success for all to see. In July 2013, CA had finalised a pathfinding broadcasting deal, under which its old confederate, the Nine Network, broadcast international cricket and new pal Ten took on the revamped Big Bash League. So not only could Australians savour England's immolation in the Ashes, but they could bask in the warm glow of the BBL, for which average crowds neared 19,000 and television audiences regularly exceeded a million. Suddenly, with its free-to-air availability, T20 in Australia seemed not only to have fulfilled its potential, but to have forged a virtuous circle with international cricket. More money flooded in from ESPN's cancellation of the Champions League, which after initial promise had long languished in the IPL's shadow. The new moolah underwrote a vigorous expansion of CA's digital capabilities, so that *cricket.com.au* became a news source in its own right, narrating the interlocking stories in heady unison.

In November 2013, Queensland premier Campbell Newman opened the National Cricket Centre, the $29 million expansion of the Centre of Excellence, on the renamed Greg Chappell Drive, Albion. It was now to be the base for an ever-growing program: home not only to its existing coaching and sports science staffs, but a staging post for an Australia A squad of advanced first-class players and a 27-member National Performance Squad of promising youth—this squad being a long-held ambition of Howard's. After a review of Australian coaching programs by Rod Marsh, its coaching of coaches was also to be expanded, under Matthew Betsey and Darren Holder. Talk was earnest, hushed and crammed with acronyms: the ACPP (Australian Cricket Performance Program) was here, incorporating IPPs (Individual Player Plans) for all those PONIs (Players of National Interest);

the NPPP (National Player Pathway Project) was coming, and not to be confused with PPP (Player Payment Pool).

As empowering as on-field playing success, in fact, was the off-field strategic vindication—the sense that Jolimont was again seen as a pace-setter. Sports columnists chorused approval; marketing savants served up cricket as a case study; the Australian Institute of Sport gave CA the highest mark in the four categories of its Sport Tally ranking system, with praise for its governance reform and pathway program. Everything looked inspired. The appointment of Lehmann was no longer the decision of a panicked executive desperate to re-establish order; it was a bold and decisive intervention that had borne immediate fruit.

CA even seemed to have found a way to deal with the unpredictable humours of India, in the second half of 2013 joining forces with the England Cricket Board in a plan to reorganise governance and financial distribution at the International Cricket Council, and accommodate the limitless ambition of the BCCI's Srinivasan. CA's Wally Edwards and his English counterpart Giles Clarke shared Srinivasan's contempt for the ICC, derided its flirtations with governance reform, and were dismissive of its executive. While the 'Big Three' scheme to vote themselves primacy at the board table and exchequer falls outside my purview here, its foreshadowing in January 2014 was widely seen as another mission accomplished. Three years earlier, Australian cricket had looked befuddled and beleaguered. Now it was incarnate in the swashbuckling arch of Mitchell Johnson's moustache, the throbbing pulse of the Big Bash beat, and the swelling columns of the CA balance sheet: in 2013-14, this not-for-profit turned over nearly $300 million, distributing a third to the state associations; keeping $84 million in the bank, it also paid key management personnel more than $5 million. To the victors, the spoils.

4

States of the Games

Not everyone bought the idea of overnight renaissance. As CEO of the Australian Cricketers' Association, and also of the Federation of International Cricket Associations, Paul Marsh continued to detect at least a tension, if not a contradiction, between CA's expressed commitment to producing consistently excellent national teams and its ambitions to access a new mass market.

Marsh's membership was bemused by the 2013-14 schedule. The Ryobi Cup was condensed from a 24-match round-robin spread across the summer to a season-starting 20-match month in Sydney: with a World Cup approaching, a player inopportunely injured could go the season playing no 50-over cricket. Thirty-five games of BBL were stretched across 58 days, not concluding until 7 February, well after the end of school holidays, scheduled thus to lead in to Ten's coverage of the Winter Olympics. A hundred and twenty-five days of Sheffield Shield were squeezed into 85 days at either end of the season, the competition resuming with a new pink Kookaburra, which CA was trialling as part of their plan for a day-night Test, but which players loathed for behaving like a tennis ball in a leather case. Even the rollout was a mess: players in a Shield match at Adelaide Oval found that there were no replacements when their ball became water-logged and went out of shape.

Since September 2012, the ACA presidency had been held by the former Australian wicketkeeper Greg Dyer, trained as a lawyer and economist, and altogether more peppery than his predecessor Michael Kasprowicz. So it was that the association committed to preparing a critique of cricket in Australia, working with Gemba on a two-stage analysis—a quantitative survey of male and female players, and qualitative focus groups with the cricket public. Consistent themes emerged, echoed at member roadshows in October-November 2013. High on the list in what was entitled *State of the Game*, as it had been in the ACA's submission to the Argus Review, were patterns of selection, still felt unduly accented to potential rather than performance, and the strength of pathway competitions, widely described as of poor quality and getting worse, with the age limits in the Futures League again blamed for having forced so many senior grade players into retirement: "The ACA continues to believe that there is enormous value in having experienced players, who may never progress to state cricket, remain in cricket ... Boys playing men has been a longstanding tradition in Australian cricket which has helped produce hardened and competitive players ready for higher honours".

Topping every concern, however, was scheduling, followed by over-prioritisation of T20, which together were "negatively impacting player preparation for parts of the Test and the majority of the one-day international components of the season", creating a "significant issue for players who play predominantly long-form cricket". One of the 25 recommendations was particularly provocative: if CA stood by their "stated priority of being the number one Test nation", said the ACA, then an argument existed for effectively swapping the BBL and the Ryobi Cup in the calendar, so that the former could involve Australian players and the latter prelude the summer's one-day internationals.

There were 24 other recommendations, but it's this one about scheduling by which *State of the Game* has been chortlingly defined. Remember when the ACA wanted the BBL in October? Where would those bumper school holiday crowds have been then, eh? Yet it was less a proposal than an observation of the uneasy coexistence of competitive and commercial purposes in Australian cricket, and the content of the report was far less significant than its being undertaken at all. Not in a century had the mass of Australian cricketers vouchsafed a view about the game—indeed, had they so openly contrasted themselves with the administrative classes. "There is little or no evidence of true accountability in Australian cricket, with many administrators holding office for long periods irrespective of on- or off-field outcomes", the report stated baldly. "Contrast this with the position of players who are quickly de-selected and replaced when performances are deemed to be insufficient." As it was presented in January 2014, at the peak of Ashes pride and BBL self-congratulation, such a sentiment sounded like a gauntlet thrown down—indeed, Pat Howard made a mission of picking it up.

If the ACA viewed Australian cricket as a glass half-empty, Howard saw it as a glass completely full. *State of the Game* was "not a true reflection" of cricket and concerns about performance were "without merit", he argued in a response longer than the original document: "The state of cricket in Australia has never been stronger. The strength is evident in all areas of cricket including game development, financially, crowd attendances and media ratings." The ACA's scheduling suggestion was the first recommendation dismissed: at its primary aim of introducing "new fans to the game", Howard said, the BBL had been an "overwhelming success", succeeding also in promoting "new heroes such as Ben Dunk and Craig Simmonds [sic]". Howard was able to go along with measures to which CA had already consented, such as a slight shortening of the BBL's duration, and a final end to the age restrictions in the Futures League. But on principles, Howard gave little. Performance, he proposed loftily, was not all that counted in selection: "CA reminds the ACA that the pathway to the Australian team has been varied. Some national players have had outstanding domestic performances, some players had mediocre domestic performances before getting selected for further honours." Who among the latter and how they had fared went unelaborated.

The general get-off-my-lawn air was particularly detectable in Howard's response to the idea of cricketers having views at all. *State of the Game* had registered discontent with CA's insistence on contracted players toeing the line in public and in print: "The ability of players to speak freely with the media is limited to comments that are construed to be 'on message'. Players who raise issues that CA do not agree with are regularly spoken to and at times have been disciplined". The ACA had expressed disquiet about CA's expansion of its digital footprint through *cricket.com.au*: "With respect to the media, we have concerns with CA's increasing view that many media outlets are competitors and therefore their access to content needs to be restricted". The players, Howard retorted, should not be biting the hand that feeds: "CA allows and accepts that players, staff and administrators will say things in the media that can or will be misconstrued. The players though, like all employees, have a duty to support the game that supports them".

Paul Marsh bridled at this: CA was arrogating to itself the status of 'the game'. Nor did players see themselves as "employees": by dint of their Player Payment Pool being derived from an agreed share of revenue, they felt as partners in the enterprise. Soon after presenting *State of the Game*, Marsh in his FICA role was asked for and gave his view on the mooted Big 3 restructure of the ICC, which he called "disturbing", contrary to "the health and sustainability of the world game" and "widening the gap between rich and poor". He received a scolding SMS from Edwards, with the inference that the CEO of the ACA should not be biting the hand that feeds either. At a subsequent conference of state association CEOs, Marsh was treated so curtly that he departed early. When he left his role with the ACA to run the AFL Players' Association in June 2014, it was with a sense of unease.

None of this unease was felt at Jolimont—and, all things considered, that should not perhaps surprise us. Who would not have felt pride, even a certain hubris, after such a heady summer? And who could quibble with a system that seemed to have discovered, nurtured and promoted the two best young players in the world?

Preparing an international cricketer can be like training a thoroughbred. Identifying the potential is one thing; intuiting if and when it might be realised is quite another. At the point Australia lost the Ashes at Chester-Le-Street in 2013, David Warner was averaging less than 40 in Test cricket, Steve Smith less than 30. Warner had just regained a place lost after a suspension for his indiscretions at the Walkabout; Smith had been lucky to retain his, with two 50s in his preceding 11 innings. In fact, a tide had come in their affairs. Over the nine matches that carried Australia back to the Test top, the pair averaged 64 and 57, and compiled five and four hundreds, respectively.

Thus were prophecies fulfilled. The night 22-year-old Warner took South Africa down at the MCG in 2009 is arguably the night the country was switched on to T20; the day 18 months later he took a Test hundred off New Zealand in a losing total at Bellerive Oval made the best case yet that the formats were reconcilable. Short and stocky, Warner's neck-to-knee space allowed bowlers little margin for errors of length; he had a drive like a gut punch, a cut like a karate chop, and a competitive urge like a cage fighter's. Feeling out of sorts before the Perth Test of January 2012, he flailed a hundred in 69 balls; flirting with disaster in the Adelaide Test of December 2012, he muscled a hundred in 93 balls; he talked as he batted, and lived, with few inhibitions, and his game and personality suited the times. Only after meeting his girlfriend Candice

Falzon on Twitter did he cease using it to remonstrate with journalists and rivals.

Smith at this stage was somewhat behind Warner, having gained a Test cap earlier but being almost three years his junior. His baby face made him an incongruous presence in team photos; his homespun technique and herky-jerky movements offended aesthetic sensibilities; his record was actually less than remarkable, featuring just one first-class hundred between March 2010 and June 2013. But his avidity for opportunity was unmistakable. At training, he was an automaton, wearing coaches out with what is widely called 'work ethic'; he cultivated a sideline in leg-spin; he caught superbly. Smith was as quiet and seemingly guileless as Warner was noisy and racy, at 18 acquiring a conscientious agent, Warren Craig, and at 21 a devoted girlfriend, Dani Willis. If he lacked for a time the substance of a career, he had even then the shape of one.

Warner and Smith, then, had been the future for some time. They had played first grade aged 16, represented their state at under-17 and under-19 level, been part of Australia's under-19 World Cup squads, been participants in the Hong Kong Sixes, teammates in the Champions League and World T20, scholars at the Centre of Excellence, early recruits to the Indian Premier League.

They had chafed against the system, in contrasting ways: Warner had had to do penance for his antics at the Walkabout; Smith had missed out on a CA contract after an unsatisfactory skinfold test. Indicative of their importance was that both were rested from Australia's one-day tour of India in 2013, offering them a breather between the Ashes series. They took full advantage. So did Lehmann. He professed to identifying with each: with Warner because he "has not always conformed" and "in this respect I see some of myself in him", with Smith because he was "unorthodox" and "I was never the prettiest of players." When Lehmann's contract was extended in August 2014, his role in the harnessing of their talents was as much the reason as any: Warner was a player, he said, who had "never given me a moment's trouble"; Smith was a player who had "improved more than any I have ever worked with". Warner and Smith reciprocated Lehmann's regard, praising him for the relaxed air he had introduced to the Australian dressing room after the angst of the Arthur years.

It was clear, too, that Warner had acquired a role beyond his specialist tasks. Against England and South Africa, 'The Bull' grew into an acrid on-field presence. Some in the team were even alarmed at how far Warner was prepared to take his animosities. He seemed to know no limit, even at press conferences, to the degree that CA public affairs began holding him back, for fear he might accuse another player of "scared eyes", as he did the troubled Englishman Jonathan Trott, or another team of "sharp practice", as he did South Africa. Others saw his antics as more of an asset, a reason that other countries might not enjoy playing Australia—and that, after all, was what it was about, eh? These included his captain, Michael Clarke, who provided an inadvertent endorsement at the Gabba in December 2013 with a barb aimed at England's James Anderson shared with a million viewers via the stump microphones: "Get ready for a broken fuckin' arm."

With some made-to-measure macho posturing, his friend and familiar Shane Warne contended, Clarke came of age: "That was the moment I believe Australia saw the very competitive, tough Michael Clarke I know, and accepted him as an Australian hero." If image-conscious Clarke blanched a little publicly, Warner never did: "We set a standard where we want to go out there and play aggressive and hard cricket and not cross the line. There are some times you do nudge that line a fair bit and the odd occasion you might step over that, but you do have to realise that we're out there to win. We do like to be aggressive and sledging is a form of the game when we're out there."

Australian cricket has long had a reputation for a barbed verbal toughness; almost as long-lasting have been self-conscious attempts to distinguish the acceptable from the unacceptable. Steve Waugh's 2003 'Spirit of Cricket' manifesto expressed disapproval for sledging but deemed "banter between opponents and ourselves" integral to "the competitive nature of cricket"—which some might call a distinction without a difference. 'The line' has sufficient of a heritage to have been celebrated in song, a chorus line of Australian cricketers in Eddie Perfect's 2008 *Shane*

Warne: The Musical braying: "We never cross the line/ Calling somebody a maggot or a filthy faggot is fine."

Under Clarke's captaincy, ideas consolidated around a vague notion that references to families were off limits, although nobody was ever prepared to explain why, or their entitlement to impose this standard, or whether they always lived up to it. The impetus was the idea that it was an advantage—and that Australia 'played our best cricket' with a barbed tongue had near enough to official sanction. As an unnamed player put it in Brettig's *Whitewash to Whitewash*: "We were told by Pat [Howard] that we'd be looked after; we wouldn't be hung out to dry if we went really hard at England. That's the brand of cricket that everyone knows we have to play to be successful".

Some collateral damage was sustained—at least reputationally. Graeme Swann deemed Warner, "a very average individual". Faf du Plessis likened the Australians to "a pack of dogs". After the series in South Africa, only one opposition player came for a drink with the Australians, and captain AB de Villiers spoke of "the worst sledging I have ever copped", confirming it had impaired relations: "There was lots of personal stuff and certain guys take it in a different way. I see that it's part of the game ... but they can't expect us to be mates with them off the field then, if they get very personal". 'Personal? Us?' Australians would reply at such times, with a hint of the casuistry of Marco Materazzi insisting that he had only insulted Zinedine Zidane's sister, not his mother.

Less instinctively confrontational, Smith was clearly learning. When he was involved in a smiling exchange with Pakistan's Azhar Ali in the Second Test in Abu Dhabi in November 2014, Clarke visibly rebuked him for undue friendliness. Asked about it later, Smith hastened to disabuse his captain that he had been fraternising with the enemy. "I was actually getting into him [Azhar Ali]," said Smith, taking a leaf from Warner's manual. "We like to play good, hard, tough, aggressive cricket when we're out in the field. That's the way we like to play, so we'll continue to do that."

When in Rome...

Then, two weeks later, Rome suddenly seemed ripe for change—at least for a moment. Phillip Hughes was in a way the triplet of Warner and Smith: born between them, likewise precocious, success similarly foretold. The trio had been contemporaries at under age level; they had emerged for New South Wales in 2007; they had toured India and England together in 2013. Much has been written about the shuddering consequences of Hughes' death in a Sheffield Shield match at the SCG, in November 2014; much remains to be said. But one of its effects was to concentrate even more expectation and hope on the shoulders of Warner and Smith, both to commemorate their comrade in the instant and to re-normalise cricket life thereafter. Before the First Test against India that followed, both were as traumatised as their teammates, paling at the sight of the Adelaide Oval nets. Warner bowled; Smith tentatively took some throwdowns. Out in the middle, the former made 145 and 102, the latter 162 not out and 52 not out—powerfully therapeutic batting in a splendid Australian victory.

When Michael Clarke aggravated injuries to his back and hamstring, the pair was pushed still further forward. At the Playford Hotel on North Terrace afterwards, Clarke's deputy Haddin took a proportional step back, telling CA director Mark Taylor that in his view Smith was the natural heir to Australia's captaincy, for having "more playing years" ahead of him. Just a couple of months earlier in the UAE, Chris Rogers had been the ranking pro when Clarke and Haddin were off the field. Now Smith's stock was surging. In Clarke's absence he took the job.

There remained an argument against any automatic succession. Smith was a very young 25. By his own admission, captaining Australia had never occurred to him. He might think he was ready; but who, really, could be? Sooner or later, John Inverarity reflected, the captaincy wore its office holders out, men as strong as Steve Waugh, Ricky Ponting and Michael Clarke; eventually the same would be true of Smith. Why not delay that process a year or two with a caretaker? If not a Haddin, it could be the self-effacing Tasmanian George Bailey, who had enjoyed rave reviews while standing in for Clarke in one-day cricket. "He's just one of those blokes you want around," said Mitchell Johnson. "He gives his all with a smile on his face but is as tough as nails." But Bailey was no longer around, having been dropped from the Test side, and Inverarity was no longer a selector, having not had his contract renewed by Howard, with whom he had not always seen eye-to-eye: on board with Rod Marsh had come previous chairman Trevor Hohns and Steve Waugh's brother Mark. As with Clarke, Taylor played kingmaker. And in Clarke's three-Test absence, the *pro tem* captain compiled three hundreds. Michael who?

It's possible that Clarke's noblest hour as Australian cricket was in the gravest circumstance. During his note-perfect eulogy at Hughes' funeral in Macksville on 2 December, he looked less a captain than a true leader, with healing words for a broken time. There followed perhaps the most mysterious phase of his tenure, all the subterranean intrigue about his fitness for the upcoming World Cup, with Shane Warne close enough almost to be Clarke's alter ego.

Warne had been an early advocate for Lehmann, in 2011 saying he would be "the perfect coach" for Australia, in 2013 promoting him again as a "great man manager" in his 'Warniefesto' for the restoration of cricket greatness, published on his personal website. But Warne's tolerance of coaches has always been limited, and he restated his position in January 2015 in a wide-ranging interview deprecating Lehmann's influence on the team, with its starting point the sight of the coach relaying Australia's declaration during the Boxing Day Test: "It was Michael Clarke who taught them how to win. Darren Lehmann has come in and put a bit of icing on the cake, he's actually complemented Michael Clarke. He's got to be a little bit careful that he's got to stop walking out on the MCG and declaring. He's got to remember that's the captain's job not the coach's job."

To this stage, Lehmann had enjoyed a remarkably good run with the media, content to present him as a stock character: *good old Boof, loves a beer, loves a fag, loves his boys.* He certainly loved some, and as a selector was positioned to act on his preferences. He had exercised his authority in the backroom, too, with bowling coach Craig McDermott, fielding coach Greg Blewett, strength and conditioning coach Damian Mednis and psychologist Michael Lloyd all joining the set-up with Lehmann's blessing. In the ranks, there existed a genuine fondness for Lehmann, with all his roughhouse ways, from the stylistic eccentricities of the emails he signed as 'Coach' to his anxious reappearance in the dressing room after his regular smokos ("Did I miss anything?"). But he was also known to miss home, sleep poorly, eat badly—and was there something a little jarring about a coach with a beer in his hand almost as soon as his players left the field? While the media obsessed with Clarke's fitness, some in the team brooded on Lehmann's. Not that there was great sympathy for Clarke, with his kvetching by proxy.

But Lehmann, tired, sometimes disarmingly sensitive and burdened by summer's emotion, was hurt by Warne's criticism—the great bowler has a way, even now, of locating vulnerabilities.

It came right. With Clarke and Lehmann back in harness for the final against New Zealand, the Australians lived up to their status as hosts and top-ranked ODI team—Warne was there with the microphone, full of good cheer. At the after party in the Harrison Room at the MCG, Sutherland and Edwards were seen jumping around the lectern with Lehmann like excited schoolboys—and little wonder. With the Cup came a colossal cash windfall, CA's share of the event's profit exceeding $50 million. From annual revenue of $380 million, more than $100 million was routed to the state associations. So great was the bounty for players and umpires—$77 million—that members of the Australian Cricketers' Association forewent $15 million to endow a player wellbeing and welfare program.

Compared to the wave of emotion that had swept through a victorious India four years earlier, however, public enthusiasm Down Under was muted. By the following weekend, the MCG was hosting the AFL and the winning cricketers were involved in the IPL alongside another eight of their countrymen. Beaten finalist New Zealand arguably emerged with more admirers. After Phillip Hughes' death, their captain Brendon McCullum had spoken every bit as movingly as Clarke. They had striven during the Cup to be generous and welcoming co-hosts—which the Australians, oddly, had found unpardonable. In a radio interview after the final, Haddin explained that his confrontational mode behind the stumps had been a riposte to the New Zealanders having been too hospitable during the round-robin. He was paying them back, as it were, in the opposite coin:

> You know what? They deserved it. They were that nice to us in New Zealand and we were that uncomfortable. I said in the team meeting: 'I can't stand for this anymore, we're going at them as hard as we can.' It was that uncomfortable… they were was that nice to us for seven days. I said, 'I'm not playing cricket like this. If we get another crack at these guys in the final I'm letting everything [out].

When Haddin was chided for this cock-eyed logic, Lehmann rushed to his wicketkeeper's defence: "He's copped a bit, hasn't he? We like to play our game, no-one got reported out of the game, so we must have played it fair. It was a little bit disappointing, but people are entitled to their opinions and you're going to have good and bad times. You accept that, and you move on." Or maybe you don't.

The mood in the Australian team as it reassembled in the Caribbean afterwards was tangibly flat and listless, even among those who had rested. The adrenalin that had carried the team forward after Hughes' death had dissipated with victory in the World Cup. With his pregnant wife Kyly at home and his talismanic friend

Warne otherwise engaged, Clarke holed up in his digs every night, subsisting on a diet of room service and *Sons of Anarchy*. Lehmann, likewise, seemed prematurely jaded. It was hard to question a captain and a coach involved in recapturing the Ashes and the World Cup in the preceding 18 months. And that was a problem.

Generals famously always fight the last war; so, for the 2015 away Ashes, did Australia's selectors. Experience having paid dividends in 2013, they went back for more, choosing from the Sheffield Shield 35-year-old Adam Voges and 33-year-old Fawad Ahmed. But only Rogers, among the old stagers, maintained standards in England: and for him, Haddin, Watson and Harris, the series was to be a last hurrah, while Johnson and Siddle would muster only seven further Tests. So much, in fact, for the Argus Review's injunction to implement effective succession planning.

Conspicuous by his absence from the routs of Edgbaston and Trent Bridge, the old sweat Haddin presented a particularly sore case. Since Hughes's death, he had presented as the most ardent of baggy green disciples, prepared to be both martyr and boor in the name of the team. Now, having excluded himself from the Lord's Test for family reasons—grave and chronic illness to his daughter—he had found his way back controversially blocked by his deputy Peter Nevill. Criticism again unsettled Lehmann, more vulnerable than he seemed. Clarke, who once would have been all over the issue, seemed strangely detached from the decision: "I don't think the selectors expected the emotional side. They thought that because Boof had talked to some of the senior players and they said they understood then it would be completely fine with the entire group." Clarke himself was plagued: by his back, his legs, his tentative bat and his overtaxed mind. By the time his wife and Warne arrived, he was raging against the dying of the light only in the pages of Sydney's *Daily Telegraph*. In private, he loitered palely, wondering how much toll the loss of Hughes had taken. "Since his death," he mused, "I'm not sure I've loved cricket in the same way." Of the team brushed aside at Edgbaston and Trent Bridge, the same might have been wondered.

5

The Australian Way

A s Clarke bade farewell to the field and Australia to the Ashes, there was cause for reflection. Fourteen years had elapsed since Australia's last win in England. Under Pat Howard's oversight, the team had developed a hybrid character, as backyard bullies and foreign fainthearts: since 2012 they were unbeaten at home, but had won only once away. Soul-searching ensued. Though Howard denied a "wholesale review" was needed and insisted that "the overall system is in good shape", he was concerned. Flatter first-class wickets mandated from 2013, for instance, had led to higher domestic scores. But as Australia's dismissal for 60 before lunch on the first day of the Fourth Test at Nottingham showed, no team in the world was quite so fragile when the ball deviated from its flight path. Where was the Goldilocks point at which everything would be 'just right'?

The zeal for experimentation in Australian cricket, however, was by now a source of disquiet. The most notable casualty was the Sheffield Shield, squeezed to the edges of seasons, banished to provincial grounds, and, with official approval, involving ever younger squads. The Shield is little understood, even by the cricket public, who see sparsely-attended and poorly-reported matches as of little consequence. Yet the competition is just a decade younger than the Ashes, and has been fought for with great esprit de corps. The benchmark team of the last decade has been Victoria, who have won it half the time—a record that in a higher-profile sports competition would be considered nearly monopolistic. For their trouble, Victorians have been regarded as a bit hard-nosed, unfashionably coached by Greg Shipperd and Andrew McDonald, uncompromisingly represented by the likes of Cameron White, Chris Rogers, John Hastings, Scott Boland, Dan Christian and Bob Quiney. Its dressing room's cult object is the John Scholes Award, named for a stalwart coach, where players vote 3, 2 and 1 for the one among them who has done most for the team cause—White, famously, will never give three votes when the team loses. Where the Vics were concerned, others often had a parrot cry: 'But they don't produce Australian

Test players.' Of course, they did, and do: by providing consistently tough opposition, they have done more than any state to maintain the general standard of the first-class competition. It was a measure of how alienated Australian cricket was becoming that it understood its first-class teams merely as factories, 'producing' cricketers like widgets to be counted, rather than as a community—organic, interactive, a place of cumulative and individual striving, where values about teams, culture, rivalry and collective endeavour were passed on patiently, as one generation mingled with the next.

Yet even among state CEOs, there was a growing reluctance to protect the Shield's integrity as a competition in its own right. It was de rigueur to talk of the Shield as concerned merely with the manufacture of individual cricket units, and winning it as a mere 'by-product', like flue gas or mine tailings. Look at David Warner and Steve Smith. Hadn't they more or less by-passed the Shield?

The competition increasingly fell prey to tinkering and dickering. In 2014-15, Howard changed its points system to "encourage more attacking batting and bowling", introducing bonuses for runs made beyond 200 and for each wicket in the first hundred overs of first innings. Except in terms of flattering Australia's more-attacking-than-thou pretensions, it was not obvious why this fiddling was important; nor did it do much to promote resilience or merit, enabling South Australia to achieve consecutive top two finishes despite losing half their games, largely because they enjoyed the benefit of a quick outfield.

In 2015-16, off the back of Australia's failure in England, and with the approach of the inaugural day/night Test at Adelaide Oval, there came a further rush of ideas for the Shield, including the use of multiple balls: the traditional red Kookaburra, the red Duke ball to simulate conditions in England, and two different Kookaburra pink balls for a taste of floodlit cricket. A match in February between NSW and WA was relocated to New Zealand, which Australia was shortly to tour, for familiarisation purposes: in the event, only three Australian players, and one batsman, were available for the tamely-drawn game in Lincoln. There were bemusing mid-game player substitutions, for vaguely articulated reasons, or to meet a claimed urgency: Victoria fielded a total of 13 players against Tasmania at the MCG, in order that Marcus Stoinis could fly to Auckland to join the one-day squad and James Pattinson the Test squad, while Western Australia's injury-prone Nathan Coulter-Nile was subbed out of a match at the WACA after three days for Joel Paris. Coulter-Nile had not long before accomplished the noteworthy feat of selection for a Boxing Day Test having not played a Shield match in nine months.

Such caprices were no more than first grade clubs had grown used to during the high-performance suzerainty, with the phenomenon of Friday afternoon briefings from state talent managers about how and where pathways players could be used on weekends. As data nets widened, more or less any pace bowler clocking 135km/h was subject to centralised workload management, which included deliveries bowled during training sessions. A club coach who had picked a promising quick might then learn that he could not be used because of state practice the following day. There was a celebrated case of a young pace bowler selected in a first grade match who it was learned would be allowed to bowl one ball. When stakes were higher, the results could be even more galling. In the aforementioned Shield match, Paris, fit and fresh, bowled like the wind, and cruelled Queensland's whole season by costing them a finals berth.

The talk was of youth, always youth, smothering young players with 'opportunity'. The innovation most reviled was the Cricket Australia XI—a team coached by national talent manager Greg Chappell, added to the Matador BBQs One-Day Cup in October 2015 and composed of players excluded from their states' best XIs, with a predominance of inclusions from the National Performance Squad. "We know we've got the talent," Howard claimed. "And we want to be able to expose these players to more high-pressure game time to help the states and to help the overall national cause." Not since the concoction of the Futures League has a concept proven so uniformly unpopular among the players, who saw elite cricket as a privilege not a right, who saw the CA XI offering individuals unearned opportunity rather than being encouraged to build a team for success.

Despite Chappell's confidence that the team would push the states, it would win just two games out of 18.

The flipside of the obsession with the new was a contempt for the old: players sensed that once they hit 30 they were half an ordinary season from the chop. Clint McKay, for two years Australia's most consistent one-day bowler, was discarded at 30, and axed by Victoria after five more first-class matches, for not being fast enough. Mark Cosgrove, Australia's most consistent first-class batsman through the first half of the decade, was cut by South Australia aged 31, for not being fit enough. Both have since prospered in county cricket. For those with the memory, it was all rather reminiscent of the inception of the Futures League, implemented with the alacrity of the Soviet scientist determined to repeat the experiment until the right result was achieved.

Howard's advocates saw him as a Billy Beane, a challenger of the pieties; detractors regarded him as an Alden Pyle, Graham Greene's quiet American, bringing disaster on the innocents with indisputable sincerity. He was assuredly mercurial. He could be the analyst supreme, rejoicing in data points, that so-and-so took such-and-such per cent of wickets with balls hitting the stumps, that beyond this degree of lateral flexion the fast bowling back was at risk. Yet he was also prone to gusts of emotion, and half-thought-through plans of entangling complexity. He was engaging, zealous, took responsibility, backed his people; he could also be unpredictable, obtuse and indiscreet, capable of letting four things slip you shouldn't know in the course of not answering another question. The impression spread that Howard was bored with stability, infatuated with novelty. Early in 2016, for example, the Australian team parted company with batting coach Di Venuto, liked and trusted, for the sake of a few dollars; Howard then threw a bunch of cash at Muttiah Muralitharan to train with the Australians ahead of their tour of Sri Lanka in July 2016. Lehmann loyally reported that Murali was a "fantastic coach" who had been "fantastic round the guys".

This fantasticity was not contagious.

For CA, the loss of the 2015 Ashes was also a marker. It came five years to the week of the inaugural Australian Cricket Conference that had heralded groupwide transformation. Yet of those who had led that change only McKenna remained. Jones, Kino and De Bohun, probably the organisation's three sharpest minds, had departed; likewise, Geoff Allardice, the phlegmatic Victorian opening batsman turned conscientious general manager of operations. The balance of the board were outsiders; the mining executive David Peever was shortly to succeed the retiring Edwards as chairman. The death of the former South Australian premier John Bannon, a true cricket aficionado, was a grave loss. New inclusions were Bob Every, the septuagenarian ex-chairman of

Wesfarmers, and Michelle Tredenick, a beige corporate adviser. There was stronger continuity with the World Cup, CA having honoured an understanding it would absorb as many of the event's staff as possible: Cup chairman John Harnden, formerly CEO of the Grand Prix Corporation and Commonwealth Games, was tapped for the board; commercial manager Nick Hockley, senior legal counsel James Scanlan and Christine Harman took equivalent roles at Jolimont. Harman filled the vacancy left by Kino's departure as general counsel and company secretary despite negligible industrial relations experience and knowledge of cricket that would not have covered a postage stamp.

There remained a few long servers who remembered CA's roots, the days when there had been numerous social games of cricket, and people had skived off to watch Sheffield Shield matches at the MCG. The place could now feel more like an events management company, preoccupied with the BBL, the nightly saturnalia going from strength-to-strength, and the promotion of floodlit Test cricket, which was presented as an innovation to rival penicillin.

Cricket-y? Not so much. One day addressing staff, a story is told, James Sutherland asked who among the 150 or so actually played the game: only a few hands were raised. An Australian player visiting was mistaken for another. An experienced coach found himself explaining what premier cricket was. When the legal department formulated new guidelines around concussion specifically exempting fielders behind point from the requirement to wear helmets, a map of fielding positions had to be drawn on a white board so Harman could understand.

Yet nor was there much evidence of a new professionalism. The organisation had grown without really maturing, had lost its former intimacy without obtaining the advantages of scale. Instead, at senior levels, there was an aping of what it was imagined were the characteristics of get-ahead sporting organisations. The BBL was going to 'crush A-League'. Cricket.com.au was going to 'crush *Cricinfo*'. Sponsors found themselves treated lightly, as though their involvement was a privilege; even mild critics were treated as hostile. Cost was incurred casually. Executive general managers obsessed over their pecking order. McKenna, gilded by the success of the BBL, deported himself as first among equals, insisting on the title 'Acting CEO' whenever Sutherland was away; Ben Amarfio, colloquially 'EGM for the fan', rejoiced in the trappings of office, including breakfast cooked by his personal assistant. For all his bluster and brainstorms, Howard at least exhibited an interest in his staff's welfare and fronted up when things went wrong. Otherwise, blame was for other people. In a now jaded office building, space pressures were ever more acute. Amarfio's burgeoning digital section, for example, abutted CA's public affairs unit. As the former naturally inclined to eavesdropping, the latter had to begin taking sensitive calls out of the office. Yet Amarfio would also inflict petty indignities such as staff having to sign out when they simply wished to move their car.

Lower level employees, frequently dedicated, sank or swam, usually out, the attitude on high being that, well, thousands of people wanted to work in cricket, and others could always be found. It was easier to 'get someone' than to groom them, easier for the disenchanted to move on than wait for advancement. Promising careers stalled, wasting talent; excellent individuals quit, disrupting stakeholder relations. The human resources function was a dead letter. Marianne Roux, a meeting-aholic, departed, unmourned. She was succeeded by a left-field pick, Alex Wyatt, whose amorphous title of executive general manager, strategy, government and people resulted in the nickname 'executive in charge of the third floor'.

A former Rhodes Scholar and McKinsey consultant recruited from a Chinese clean energy company, Wyatt was more at home writing papers on high-level strategy than dealing with the minutiae of workplace frictions. In his favour was both a brilliant mind and a cricket sensibility: he played for Deepdene United CC in Melbourne's Eastern Cricket Association. But that became an issue in December 2014 when Wyatt incurred a heavy suspension for an on-field confrontation in a club game, remaining strangely impenitent when the story came to light. He was gone within a year, followed by his HR manager Belinda Bacon.

On this, now into a 15th year as CEO, Sutherland

rather closed his door, guarded by personal assistant Anne Lewis. Even to long-term colleagues, he remained something of an enigma. Having spent his life in leafy suburbs and worked his way up so quickly, his personal and professional experience was actually not that broad, and his education merely an undergraduate degree in commerce until he took an executive management course at Stanford. He tended to attract admiring rather than intimate friends, and preferred external advisers to internal counsel: Colin Carter, Don Argus, Peter Collins from the Centre for Ethical Leadership, Professor George Foster from Stanford, Rohan Sajdeh from Boston Consulting. Formal and reticent, he liked men to wear ties in the office, was thought to prefer email to direct contact; he never discovered ease with the media and could be sensitive to criticism.

The irony is that by other measures CA had on his watch become far more progressive and inclusive, espousing an ethos of 'A Sport for All'—a cause to which Sutherland, father of two boys and a girl, was sincerely committed. The 2013 broadcast rights deal allowed the endowment of significant participation initiatives among Indigenous and multicultural communities, building on worthy but piecemeal activities in the past. The Indigenous Imparja Cup was reconfigured as a fully-fledged national championship. All abilities cricket—for the deaf, the vision impaired and the intellectually impaired— was consolidated in the National Cricket Inclusion

Championships. In February 2015, most significantly, CA foreshadowed a Women's Big Bash League paralleling the men's—Sutherland's daughter Annabel at age 15 would become its youngest player.

The fifth season of the BBL was by far its most successful, crowned by a crowd of 80,883 for a local derby at the MCG between the Stars and Renegades in January, 2016. Indeed, it rather overshadowed the lacklustre international summer. Yet Sutherland's long tenure had by now become problematic, partly because of what it implied about management depth. Could it really be true that he had been the individual best-qualified to run cricket in Australia for all that time, and still was? Into the vacuum that nature abhors, a new presence expanded, by unique means: an independent director for the last three years, Kevin Roberts was encouraged to replace Wyatt on the executive, and identified at once as Sutherland's likeliest successor.

Since leaving adidas, Roberts had had rather a chequered corporate career, leading two troubled companies, the footwear firm Colorado and the athletic brand 2XU. He presented, nonetheless, as extremely polished, at home in every room—a contrast to Sutherland's deadpan mien. He was entrusted, too, with a high-profile project—a Wyatt initiative, OneTeam, which sought to integrate the state associations more thoroughly with CA, beginning with the consolidation of certain back office functions. Rather like Steve Smith the year before, Roberts had burst from the pack to become the anointed one. Both would find the rest of the journey less smooth.

W ith Clarke's retirement post-the 2015 Ashes, leadership of the Australian team devolved at last to Steve Smith and David Warner—a remarkable rise for young men who two years earlier had been unsure of their places in the side. It now seemed to make sense. Smith, as we have seen, had been the dauphin since the summer before. Warner? He had filled in as vice-captain during the Arthur era, not, with his bumptious demeanour, to universal approval; with that in mind, he had quietly dedicated himself to looking the part for the previous year. Widely excoriated for a confrontation with India's Rohit Sharma ("Speak English! Speak English!") in a one-day international at the SCG in January 2015, he had toned down his behaviour, giving several interviews where he cheerfully owned that his team nickname of 'The Bull' had been jokingly softened to 'The Reverend'; he had also earned rave reviews for captaining Sunrisers Hyderabad to victory in IPL7.

Captaincy is the most mythologised of cricket's faculties. The skills compound required, of individual excellence, tactical acumen, interpersonal skill and public diplomacy, is also unique to the game: there is no counterpart to Mike Brearley's *The Art of Captaincy* in any other team sport. Yet it is also not something that cricket teaches well.

Corporate leader Don Argus had been intrigued by this deficiency, and proposed, naturally, a corporate solution: he had CA introduce Michael Clarke to an American CEO consultant, Stephen Miles, to what consequence it is hard to determine.

Historically, captaincy has been learned at lower levels. Australian skippers have come to the job with prior experience at junior, grade and state levels. In more individualistic times, these opportunities were dwindling, which Howard had recognised by convening a captaincy camp in February 2014, where Mark Taylor and George Bailey were among the presenters. Less easy to teach, however, was the consideration of and curiosity about others which lies at the heart of successful leadership, especially in a system encouraging such minute monitoring of the individual, and so attuned to the priorities of the moment. Smith and Warner were elevated by their unique specialist talents, rather than ideal personalities, or, for that matter, personal affinity— and learning to lead cricket teams by captaining Australia must be thought the equivalent of learning to drive in a Formula One racing car.

One of the effects of this somewhat uneasy fit was to enhance the importance of the coach as the voice of stability and continuity. This was an issue in itself. Lehmann's health was no longer merely a dressing room talking point. In January 2016, he suffered a severe recurrence of deep vein thrombosis, which saw him hospitalised, and for a period restricted him from flying. In July, Howard insisted he have a break, and appointed a locum, Justin Langer, to coach Australia during a tri-series in the Caribbean.

Otherwise, Lehmann seemed very much ensconced. Victories against New Zealand at Wellington and Christchurch provided the team with a mathematical nudge past India in the ICC Test rankings to achieve key performance indicators and to burnish reputations. In a reshuffle of the Australian backroom caused by the departures of Di Venuto and McDermott, Greg Blewett was promoted and Victorian coach David Saker joined the team—two kindred figures unlikely to contend for the top job. In fact, as something of a quid pro quo for skipping the West Indies, Lehmann's contract was extended early, to the end of 2019 Ashes, by which time he would be pushing 50. He even began building his brand, looking to expand the private cricket academy in Unley with which he'd been connected for several years, and signing with Penguin to produce a manifesto entitled *Coach*, the *nom de guerre* he now preferred. The back cover would feature a photograph of Lehmann gesturing decisively with a straight right arm, while Steve Smith stood to one side looking even younger than usual.

By the time *Coach* was published, however, that coach-captain dynamic would appear rather different. With overwhelming defeats in Kandy, Galle and Colombo, the trend in Australia's offshore results resumed. Smith's team might have had Murali in the nets, but the Sri Lankans had a figure on the field whom the virile Australian system would have superannuated long before: Rangana Herath, a 165cm jug of a man who hailed from a remote village, had worked as a bank clerk, and not become a Test regular until his mid-30s. The Australians lurched from complacent to captious. Batsmen deprived of boundaries by slow outfields looked helpless; bowlers defending tiny totals lost patience. Among those appearing in all three Tests, Smith alone averaged 40 with the bat, and Starc alone paid less than 30 runs per wicket. With the first setbacks of his captaincy, Smith visibly wrestled, sometimes seething on the field, seemingly distrait off it, to the extent it was decided to spare him the tour's short-form leg. That rebounded upon him also. Smith reads the cricket media closely, and smarts when criticised. Reproached for returning home by Michael Clarke and Michael Slater, he watched improved Australian performances with mixed feelings.

Stand-in skippers come in two kinds. Leading Australia in one-day internationals, George Bailey was of the first sort, unassuming and easy-going, acknowledging the team as borrowed from Michael Clarke, to be returned in a similar state or better. In Sri Lanka, David Warner was far more assertive, not without cause after the team's dismal Test matches, but observably ambitious—optimistic, solicitous, encouraging, and, above all, focused, channelling his energies into providing a positive environment for teammates rather than a negative one for opponents. Now he reversed Australia's momentum, leading them to five wins in six starts, even earning praise from Bailey, who called him a "natural leader"—a permissible inference being that Warner was not so natural a follower. Warner even started sounding a little like a product ambassador: "That's how we play. That's the Australian way. We have always played that way… We like to play an aggressive brand of cricket. We like to entertain the crowd".

Such self-praise never entirely goes out of fashion in this country; but there was now something of an uptick in references to an approved 'Australian way', tapping into what was seen as an innate aggression that been allowed to attenuate. Partly this was an attempt to stamp a personality on a team suddenly seeming a little short of it; partly it reflected Lehmann's own disposition, harkening to an imagined past where Australia outbowled, outbatted and outswore all comers. Lehmann liked kicking around ideas like "moving the game on", "positive body language", "getting in a contest", "being in their faces" while also, of course, not 'crossing the line'. In a presentation he evolved for other coaches about 'the Australian Way', he mentioned a "team philosophy" of "aggression and freedom going forward" and discussed exhorting players to be "aggressive in everything you do!" This encompassed the way they talked about the game: "WTBC" read his opening slide, an abbreviation of "Watch the ball, cunt".

Warner was an instant recruit: he revelled in the role of "keep[ing] our guys motivated on the field". Potential was also discerned in keeper Matthew Wade, out of Test calculations for three years, but a limited-overs regular, inconsistent with the gloves but consistent in his pugnacity. When Smith rejoined the squad for a one-day series in South Africa, Australia floundered again, choosing a second-string attack to allow the first to recharge for the home summer. But Warner excelled, flailing 386 runs from 342 balls in five hits, and audible, visible and fricative on the field; Wade made spirited runs on the one occasion Warner failed.

Teammates had always joked about an undertone of rivalry between Smith and Warner—how if one scored a hundred, a hundred from the other was seldom far away. Now there was more to it. When *Coach* was published, Lehmann was complimentary of Smith, whom he deemed the player who had "improved more than any other I have ever worked with", but unqualified in his endorsement of Warner: "He plays the game in exactly the way I want, taking on the opposition, putting them under pressure from ball one and seeking to dictate the course of the match"; "For me, he really has become a leader, including what he does off the field." Warner's excesses, meanwhile, were minimised: his confrontation with Rohit Sharma, for example, was to Lehmann "just the tail-end of some chat that had been going on for a while". Elsewhere there were mutterings: that

Smith, barely accustomed to the job, already had cause to feel vulnerable; that Lehmann's position in this was ambiguous. Things would get worse before getting better—and then, of course, infinitely worse.

Their confidence damaged by five one-day defeats away in South Africa, the Australians sustained consecutive Test defeats to the same opponents at home. A far stronger Australian team had suffered a similar fate eight years earlier, but following the fiasco of Sri Lanka, such setbacks now qualified as a crisis, to the extent of involving an unprecedented visit to the dressing room at Bellerive Oval by both Howard and Sutherland: "the suits", as Smith would call them, with the same dread as a schoolboy might refer to the headmaster. "It's not something I'd ever experienced before in my career," Smith recalled, "and I hope it's not something I'll ever experience again." Five consecutive Test defeats was not good enough, warned Sutherland from his great height, looming over the deflated players. There would be changes, he said; there had already been several. The first step in a hoped-for new era looked like a harbinger. When chairman of selectors Rod Marsh stood down, remarking that it was "time for fresh thinking", Howard ignored other names advanced and reappointed … Greg Chappell.

For so long the Argus Review's most ardent apostle, Howard now flew in its face. Five years earlier Argus had prised the national talent manager from the selection panel on grounds that choosing and grooming new cricketers were activities necessarily discrete from international selection. On the panel henceforward would now be not one but two proponents of the pathway program, as Trevor Hohns was talent manager for Queensland. A third, Mark Waugh, was both a television commentator and the long-time 'governor' of the Sydney Thunder. With six changes, the selectors heeded Sutherland's mandate. Out: Joe Burns, Joe Mennie and Callum Ferguson after single Tests, the injured Mitchell Marsh, plus recent regulars Adam Voges and Peter Nevill. In: uncapped Nic Maddinson, Matthew Renshaw, Peter Handscomb, and Chadd Sayers, plus Jackson Bird and Matthew Wade. A football team making so many changes would have been viewed as in disarray, and there were some grounds for bafflement.

Shortly to turn 25, Maddinson was every inch the system cricketer. A prodigy from Nowra, he had represented his state at under-17 and under-19 level, earned 15 Australian under-19 caps, played a dozen Futures League matches, taken three Australia A tours. But despite rare power and phases of looking the part, the promise Maddinson had exuded in scoring two first-class hundreds at 18 had not been fulfilled: in six home first-class seasons, he had averaged over 40 once and less than 30 thrice. Ripe fruit? Or something picked for being the right shape and flavour? Discarded by Australia after three unsuccessful Tests, Maddinson would, two years later, be axed by his state.

The selectors' signature call, however, was probably the

axing of the undemonstrative Nevill in favour of the ornery Wade—a palpable investment in the perceived 'Australian way'. Arguably not the third best gloveman in Australia, Wade had been pressing his claims by moving himself up the order for Victoria, but the clinching argument in his favour was Smith's regard for his being "vocal on the field" and "willing to get stuck in". In 10 Tests over the next year, Wade would be vocal, stick in and average 20—ironically as his glovework showed some solid improvement.

It wasn't verbal prowess that took the fight to the Proteas at Adelaide Oval. Rather was it the quietly-spoken Usman Khawaja, whose hand-crafted century spanned nearly eight hours. But Smith proceeded to double down on his new keeper when Glenn Maxwell, in the course of a standard issue press conference for Victoria a few days later, let slip that it had been "a bit painful" to bat lower in the order than Wade in the Shield as he sought his own opportunities. CA saw no reason to discipline Maxwell for his anodyne comments; in an unusual step, the Australian leadership group, composed at the time of Smith, Warner, Starc and Josh Hazlewood, levied on their occasional colleague an undisclosed fine for being "very disrespectful". Smith then revealed this exclusively to *cricket.com.au*. This heavy-handed, self-serious interlude seemed as much about indulging Smith, helping him place his hallmark on the captaincy, as protecting Wade, who as he was so tough could presumably look after himself. Maxwell next suffered the indignity of acting as

12th man throughout a three-match Chappell-Hadlee Trophy series, as though wearing his own personal pillory.

Australia had a better time of it as summer wore on, Smith and Warner piling up 800 runs between them and Handscomb and Renshaw securing maiden hundreds in three successful Tests against a spasmodic Pakistan; batsmen then peeled off five hundreds in five one-day internationals. But the propensity of certain cricketers to offer actual opinions rather than to obediently 'support the game that supports them' was growing into a source of vexation at Jolimont.

In 2015-16, player concerns had revolved around day/night Test cricket and the quality of the pink ball, complained of by Voges, Starc, Hazlewood and John Hastings. Sutherland, irked, had dismissed such complaints as "too late", insisting that "our players just need to focus on what's ahead." In 2016-17, tension emerged over scheduling, when CA slotted in T20 internationals against Sri Lanka for which Test players would be rendered unavailable by a Test in India. Exactly what was 'Australia' when two teams of that name were effectively on duty at once? Just another brand name in the portfolio, like 'Sydney Sixers' or 'Hobart Hurricanes'? David Warner stuck his head above the parapet on *Fox Sports* to lament the "very, very poor scheduling", and argue that "you want to be putting your best team on the park all the time". This time, CA kept its own none-too-happy counsel.

Finally, selection reared its head. When Maddinson was followed by Hilton Cartwright, was followed by Billy Stanlake, was followed by Sam Heazlett, effectively on pathways promise crossed with BBL form, Victoria's Cameron White, a former Australia T20 captain now regarded as the dean of domestic cricket, voiced concerns in a radio interview: "For me, playing for Australia isn't about giving you a chance to develop. Domestic cricket is where that happens, and Futures League. I just want to see the best players playing". More circumspect than Warner, White couched his words respectfully. He was "just a little worried". He was "not against young players playing at all". He decried no specific selection, ignored his having played a single one-day international in five years despite dominating domestic one-day cricket—in which Heazlett, by contrast, had never even represented his state. In replying, chairman Hohns did not match this note of moderation:

> I'm a little bit surprised by those comments, to be quite honest. The Sheffield Shield has been well-documented as being very important to us in Australian cricket— selectors, everybody. And then younger players— I think he [White] just needs to remember that he was a very young man when he was given his first opportunity in one-day cricket. I don't think there is any disparity there at all, to be honest. Cameron has had plenty of opportunities ... He has had plenty of opportunities in the past and it's probably fair to say performed okay without being earth-shattering.

The interlude came on the eve of a meeting between representatives of CA and the Australian Cricketers' Association, attempting to revive desultory discussions about their next collective bargaining agreement. Hohns's comments derailed it. When the ACA's CEO Alistair Nicholson told Pat Howard that he felt that Hohns had been "disproportionate" in his retort, Howard began plucking numbers from the air to back Hohns up. That was not the point, Nicholson insisted: what right did Hohns have to "belittle a former Australian captain in a public forum"? The meeting concluded with the parties as far apart as ever—and that, some already sensed, was the point.

6

Smash the Boundaries

'The players': through 2017, as negotiations of their collective agreement with Cricket Australia roiled, they were the talk of Australian cricket. 'The players' wanted this. 'The players' would not accept that. 'The players' drove Lamborghinis—well, one of them did, and David Warner was in many eyes an archetype, even if he was more realistically an exception. It makes more sense to think of a collective of cricketers than it does of footballers: the Australian Cricketers' Association has 300 current male and female playing members compared to the AFL Players' Association's more than 1000. Yet within that are many gradations—of age, aptitude, locality, background, gender, wealth. Then there are the marked separations of experience. There is no team in Australia like its Test cricket team, first chosen from a clutch of colonies containing barely two million people, and still sporting the colours first worn before Federation. No national side is considered so representative; no national side is quite so elevated and sequestered from those whom they represent.

The players know it, too. Back in the palmy days of the early 21st century, those at Cricket Australia charged with responsibility for dealing with the Australian cricket team spoke of an iron law. For their first 15 Tests and/or 30 one-day internationals, an Australian cricketer would be good as gold—excited, obliging, grateful, and generally happy to be there. After that, negotiations became complicated.

The cricketer would grow expectant, entitled, maybe even a bit surly, harder to persuade to do anything not directly or indirectly related to playing, tending towards the bare minimum of cooperation. In part this was a response to their privileged status; in part also was it a kind of husbanding of energies in the face of a career's demands. We think of cricketers in terms of their on-field performances, of the effort expended in a marathon spell or a giant innings. But the bulk of their time is future-focused, the work that goes to the all-consuming analysis of performance, minuscule adjustments of technique, tiny enhancements in physical prowess, and a general coming to terms with ceaseless scrutiny, both energising and enervating.

Cricket becomes not the most important thing in life; it is life. As one adjusts to that regime, so one must economise elsewhere, guarding one's diminishing sphere of personal autonomy more jealously. Does the 15/30 rule still apply? A form of it must. Why? Precisely because *not* to be changed by the experience would be abnormal. And the best way to think of the Australian dressing room is an extraordinary setting for a group of men otherwise quite ordinary—except for their preternatural giftedness in a certain narrow but highly-valued set of specialist skills.

In the course of writing *Crossing the Line*, I spoke to a score of people with experience of Australian dressing rooms during Darren Lehmann's tenure. Away from the life, in repose, there was actually a strong sense of its unreality, the luxurious trappings of the pointy end of planes, plush apartments and comfortable lounges. The best-paid players earn more than $1 million a year—some have earned millions more from the IPL. For all his fealty to the All Blacks, Pat Howard made no effort to introduce those aspects of its culture that are famously grounding— the strong attachment to heritage, the 'sweep-the-sheds' belief that the team should look after itself ("Never be too big to do the small things that need to be done"). To join the Australian team is to have things done for you. With the best will in the world, it is hard not to be caught up in that.

In return, one submits to days managed in the minutest degree. Schedules, messages and resources that used to be slipped beneath the hotel room door now arrive via an app from CA's Athlete Management System (AMS)—an efficient distribution means, as most players are inseparable from their phones.

The AMS makes reciprocal demands, requiring a constant feed of data from the player about their activity, welfare, recent performances, future objectives. Its dashboard presents eight options accented to playing and training workloads, calibrated minutely. If a player has batted on a certain day, for example, they must account for the elapsed time and balls faced, and whether the activity was "very easy", "easy", "moderate", "moderately hard", "very hard", "very, very hard", "extremely hard", "sub-maximal" or "maximal".

A wellness section requires inputs about sleep, soreness, stress and fatigue. "How do you rate your fatigue?" the app asks with quiet insistence: are you "always tired", "more tired than normal", "normal", "fresh" or "very fresh"? Other pages survey "reflections", on training and on games. Did the player have a "Clear Plan"? Did the player "Stick to the Plan"? How had they gone "Creating a Contest"? Did they achieve "Focus" and "Execute Skills"? One tiny box on this screen strikes a plaintive note: "Enjoyment". Players complete the foregoing dutifully, albeit as much because of the consequences of not doing so. "I fill in my AMS so the S & C [strength and conditioning coach] and the physio don't get in trouble," says a Test player. "But it's just more rope to hang yourself by."

Developed by Microsoft, CA's Athlete Management System app also contains two self-reporting features related to psychic wellness: every male and female player in the elite system must monitor their EPQ (Eysenck Personality Questionnaire), an inventory of character traits, and K10 (Kessler Psychological Distress Scale), an index of depression and anxiety. Whether the resources exist to make the feedback effective is difficult to say. The story is told of a female player who fell behind her K10 requirements because she was depressed—she received a call admonishing her for delinquency. She resumed, reporting low levels of mental wellness for the next fortnight—to … nothing. Presumably the Australian team is monitored more closely. Yet some aspects of people management remain strangely crude. The call up and/or the drop down, for example, are delivered by phone, briskly, sometimes brusquely.

"At the moment, it's like this," says an experienced player. "Cracker [Trevor Hohns] calls and says: 'You're dropped.' You say: 'OK, what do I do?' He says: 'Just do what you're doing now, go out and make heaps of runs and take heaps of wickets.' And that's it. They feel no duty of care. They're thirty years behind the AFL in that respect. I'm OK. I've been through disappointment and I've learned to handle it. But the next generation isn't like that. They take it really hard."

It is a life without a real centre. Footballers roll in at their clubs every day, and travel no further than darting interstate. Australian cricketers are always in transit.

Tours are shorter than they were, but further away, more frequent and more restricted. The days of testosterone-fuelled maraudings are mainly past, thanks to the frequent presence of players' wives and girlfriends, leavening the environment's artificiality. Yet this can cut both ways, pinning players to their hotels, while breaking the team up when it might be regrouping. "It doesn't feel normal when they're not there," noted a well-travelled tourist. "But it sometimes doesn't feel normal when they're there either. I've been lucky. I have loved having my wife with me, but I've seen it hurt teams too. When you're overseas and hotel bound, you get back from a day and you're smothered by your family. Your wife is bored, your kids are awake; you are not debriefing, attending to a few of your own worries, in that informal way that often gets a lot more done."

While the life seems exotic, it is also strangely sterile. Australia's cricketers visit more countries than 99 per cent of their countrymen, but seldom see other than cricket grounds and hotel rooms, obliged to visit the former, discouraged by security from leaving the latter, locked into a relentless cycle of practice-practice-play-recover that leaves little spare time and energy. This being so, they can seem underwhelming. "They know a fair bit about cricket, although not as much as you might think," said a former member of the Australian support staff. "They know a lot about movies. Can identify a line from a movie like 'that'. Because that's what they do: they play cricket, they go to their rooms to watch movies. They could tell you the

Prime Minister's name, because they go to his place every year. But the Opposition Leader? Probably not. About the countries they visit they're amazingly ignorant." Yet in a way, this could hardly be otherwise. The sailor's home is not the sea but the ship. Think of them as our most cossetted fly-in-fly-out workers, with similarly handsome rewards and attendant insecurities—of the latter perhaps even more. For the fall, when it comes, as eventually it must, will hurt. Every political career, it has been said, ends in failure; the same is true of cricket careers. Perhaps that's necessary. Otherwise they might not end at all.

D arren Lehmann was initially considered a relaxing relief from the careworn Arthur regime. There were no agonies about discipline. At his first team meeting, he laid out simple ground rules for Warner: "Fuck up again, Davey, and you're gone". Lehmann's bonhomie also offered a contrast to the austere English set-up of Andy Flower. You could have a beer. You could tell a joke. He was loath at first to take selectorial responsibilities, which "had the potential to create friction between the players and myself": Howard needed to persuade him. Nor did he see himself staying overlong, liking to quote his wife Andrea's question when he was offered the job: "Do you think you can make a difference?"

But Lehmann did stay. In a sense, he had to. Cricket coaching is a precarious occupation. The national role is the only one in Australia paid anything like a football coach; the position's prestige and perquisites are unmatched. In hindsight, some felt Lehmann should have moved on after the 2015 World Cup, by which time he was clearly feeling the pressure of indifferent health and prolonged separations from home. But with the retirements of Clarke, Haddin, Rogers, Harris, Johnson and Watson in short order, following the tragedy of Phillip Hughes, the coach's continuity appeared welcome. His influence was then consolidated by the need for the team's remaking under Smith and Warner, suddenly senior players despite their relative inexperience. As the coach was getting older, the players were growing younger. More and more he referred to them as "kids"—"good", "great", "hard-working" etc— when they might be men in their mid-20s or even older.

Lehmann is a coach of marked likes and dislikes, has a sentimental side and a bullying side. He can embrace, dote, protect; he can also undermine, intimidate and exclude. His preference, as far as one can ascertain it, is for a kind of talented but docile cricketer in need of guidance, and play to have an edge of abrasion. Thus that muscular ideology of the 'Australian Way', first glimpsed during Mitchell Johnson's mighty summer of 2013-14, although after 2016 without Johnson to provide a simultaneous physical threat, and not by then a natural vein for many players bar Warner and also Wade. "That stuff about 'the line'—that's Boof's baby," reported one player, adding: "The guys in the team actually don't have those sort of personalities, and they're not equipped to handle the ramifications when inevitably it goes wrong."

A curious thing even in this time, in fact, was that while the Australians could be boorish, they were arguably a bit better behaved than a good many teams of earlier generations. They built solid friendships with overseas players through various T20 leagues. They remained great applauders of opponents, and handshakers too—though it is not often mentioned, there are many more handshakes on cricket fields now than there were in days of yore. Their off-field behaviour was, generally, irreproachable, or at least discreet. The team contained some engaging and thoughtful personalities.

So when they talked about that 'line', which they constantly reconnoitred, they sounded a bit parodic, like Spinal Tap straining to impress everyone by the armadillos down their trousers. Warner, meanwhile, was doing double duty, prating to journalists about "war" and "hatred", engineering pointless confrontations on the field with opposition players perceived to be vulnerable, partly because this was what was expected of him as a "leader". An atmosphere of lenience prevailed. Criticised for his "body language" by Shane Warne, Mitchell Starc grew more demonstrative, although in doing so he looked mainly sulky. Previously a sober citizen, Josh Hazlewood began skirmishing with opponents and umpires. Previously not a sober citizen, and at the time actually suspended by his state for drunken and abusive behaviour at an official cricket function, Steve O'Keefe was whistled up for a Test in Bangladesh when Hazlewood was injured.

The cult's most improbable recruit was the hitherto genial Nathan Lyon, who in a peculiar press conference before the 2017 Gabba Test described certain English players as "scared" and talked of "ending the careers" of a few of them: "We're going to play the Australian way. We're going to compete hard … We know where the line is. We headbutt it, but we don't go over it." Other contemporary players were not uniform on the subject of Australia's intimidatory reputation, but one summed up a common sentiment: "The guys we have are good enough to win without needing to do anything like it. But we just held onto this idea that we always played this way, which we didn't."

Where was the 'spirit of cricket', that doctrine of 'fair play' meant to act as a restraint on players and a bulwark of the game's reputation, in all this? A fair question. Woolly and anachronistic a concept as it often seems, it had been a fixture in CA strategic plans for almost 20 years. But when CA released *Australian Cricket Strategy 2017-2022* in September 2017—evolved mainly by Kevin Roberts "through more than 12 months' collaboration with all parts of cricket"—the spirit had mysteriously dried up. In its place were a series of corporate vacuities:

HOW WE PLAY

Be real, smash the boundaries, make every ball count, stronger together….

Be relentless … Play to win

The 'Spirit of Cricket' was now of far less moment than "We will give the fans what they want and grow the Big Bash", which was perhaps more properly what the broadcasters wanted, and even than "We will use technology to deliver great experiences for fans, participants and volunteers", which sounded like adapting iPads as thigh pads. The CA that in 2003 had persuaded players to commit to their 'Spirit of Cricket' screed by now showed as little interest in it as the Lehmann who had then signed on to it. A respected cricket figure with concerns about the Australia team's demeanour was told by Howard to "man up"; when former Australian captain Brian Booth and all-rounder Tom Veivers wrote to the CEO voicing their concerns, Sutherland told them they had to understand that cricket was tougher than in their 1960s heyday.

Surveys undertaken for CA warned that both the 'recognisability' and the 'likeability' of the Australian team was under pressure. To this came the counterargument that the public falls most eagerly behind winners— and in the debate between nebulous notions of emotional attachment to the game and winners-are-grinners pragmatism, the latter was always likely to prevail, being what the system was geared to generate anyway. Reports of declining standards of behaviour in junior ranks, in apparent imitation of the general tone of top-level truculence, were treated derisively. Why, just look at all the happy children in their replica gear sticking KFC buckets on their heads at BBL matches. If everyone just "smashed the boundaries", it would work out fine. Wouldn't it?

Those with whom I spoke about the dressing room atmosphere in Lehmann's last couple of years felt that it fluctuated, and markedly. In India in 2017, for which the team prepared assiduously, it was cohesive and purposeful; in England for the Champions Trophy a few months later, it was flat and apathetic. It could pull together for Tests but rather dragged itself along in short-form cricket, as players were constantly turned over, as the number of games grew meaninglessly.

A visitor in that time was Lehmann's occasional relief coach and future successor, Justin Langer, who was shocked at the dressing room's degeneration, its inward focus, its pervasive hauteur. Yet that was a brittle cockiness, masking weakness and unease. A player summed up the one-day side in a word: "'Individuals'. There were no basics, no planning. You got together in the morning, went your separate ways at night. It never felt like an Australian 'team' in any sense of the word." Another player felt that Lehmann had fallen into this coaching fashion simply through running short of things to say: "I love Boof. He's got a great heart and he loves the players. But, really, he hardly coached technique at all. 'You're struggling? Just whack it.' 'You're going for runs? Just bowl yorkers.' 'We'll smash them.' He really just had no other answers but to try and build up this arrogance."

Concerns were muted, further, by a general lack of trust. If one held misgivings, to whom could one turn?

The key support staff were by now all Lehmann liegemen. Howard had created the damn system. Greg Chappell had previously been identified as a problem yet somehow worked a passage back. Mark Waugh was a figure of fun, proverbially in closer touch with the races at Wyong than form in the Shield. A player recounted: "I was watching the Big Bash League with my wife and one of the other commentators said: 'Darcy Short is going really well at the moment, isn't he, Junior?' Mark says: 'I haven't seen a lot of him.' My wife says: 'Isn't he meant to be a selector?'" There were, moreover, repercussions for those who spoke out of turn: viz Glenn Maxwell and Cameron White. Then, to heap Pelion upon Ossa, CA embarked on a futile war with the Australian Cricketers' Association.

The antecedents to the pay dispute, CA's attempt to break the revenue-sharing model by which Australian elite cricketers had been paid for nearly two decades, are not far to seek. There had long been grumbling at board level about the players sharing in the upside of Australian cricket in ways insensitive to its rising costs; this had been attended to by various carve-outs from Australian Cricket Revenue from which the Player Payment Pool (PPP) was calculated, but never quite resolved to satisfaction. As far back as 2011, the Argus Review, much concerned with "incentive systems", had entertained "moving away from a fixed share of revenue going into the PPP", while adding the qualification "if required", and eventually settling for a range of bonuses to "give greater emphasis on performance".

In 2015, CA had mooted, for the first time, a separate Memorandum of Understanding for women's cricketers, as an interim measure until their complete incorporation in the next Collective Agreement, but without proposing any addition to the PPP. 'The players', it was true, had done well from the revenue share, thanks to the game's overall growth; it was not obvious that CA had done badly, revenues for the two years to 30 June 2017 exceeding $650 million. But as a constraint on a sporting organisation that saw itself increasingly in commercial terms, and that at a senior executive level paid itself accordingly, the revenue share was ripe for challenge.

What is less well understood is that this was an ideological as much as a financial dispute. Especially since 2010's Australian Cricket Conference, CA had been effectively rationalising Australian cricket. It amounted to a fundamental change of view. The former diffusion of powers through the federal system was now seen not as democratic and representative but fragmentary, wasteful and an affront to bureaucratic tidy-mindedness; local programs and approaches demonstrated not initiative and originality, but were parochial, sectional, small. The consolidation of power at Jolimont begun by the establishment of the new board had proceeded apace. CA had bought out the states of their rights to international cricket. National approaches had been agreed in areas such as game development, sponsorship, signage, insurance, even pitches. Resources were now being poured into establishing a national media voice through *cricket.com.au*. Coaching doctrine flowed ceaselessly from the National Cricket Centre. Except that, well …

Nobody much liked the NCC. The built environment was impressive, but the pitches seemed tired, the personnel were nothing special, and the pretensions sometimes absurd (centre-wicket practice as "the Battle Zone"?). Above all it was felt to reflect Howard's obsession with reducing cricketers to numbers, even when the rankings of "2-5yr 60+ (PRT/EPQ) players" were entirely subjective, not much more than what a state talent manager reckoned. Some, too, feared young cricketers were advancing on their coachability rather than their ability, with a preference for the raw talent with 'revs', ball speed and/or 'X-factor' over the player with the sturdy technique and steady temperament; likeliest to go far was the conformist who aped the required behaviours.

CA vaunted the NCC regularly. Whenever *cricket.com.au* reported its intakes, they were hyped as 'future stars', as though their success was preordained. Yet what had the millions invested really achieved? Cricket's star recruit from football, Alex Keath, lost his way there, and returned to his former sport. Steve Smith told his coach Trent Woodhill that the most important skill he had learned in Brisbane was pretending to pay attention but ignoring everything he was told. The pathway system also seemed to fetishise the player who might "win you a game" with a timely six or a key wicket rather than the player who performed consistently or displayed resilience—because what could a coach add to them?

Youngsters certainly worked hard during their 16-week courses, to the extent that visitors would note that they looked exhausted. But they emerged, some in the state system felt, like automata: batsmen very good at smashing throwdowns between cones who might at a pinch get going every tenth innings; bowlers with gym-honed physiques and great 2km time trials but still needing coaches to tell them when their hard-won skills should be used. They also readily came away, those same observers noted, with feelings of entitlement, such as a belief in themselves as "future stars", now above the chore of club cricket—a contempt summed up in the pejorative 'clubbie'. It made a handy excuse for not performing at that level, and eventually not playing at all.

Sheffield Shield? Well, they'd play if they had to, but why take the long way when the game offered so many short cuts? "Young players aren't stupid," noted a seasoned elite cricketer. "They aren't much concerned if they miss first-class cricket. What matters is being a hundred per cent fit and raring to go for the Big Bash League because that's where they can get noticed." The system's dwindling diversity, another senior cricketer argued, was a prescription for spreading mediocrity everywhere:

> There is nothing the NCC teaches cricketers that could not be passed on by their states. As it stands, the system simply institutionalises young players further. I always thought that the strength of domestic cricket was that people were allowed to do things their own way. When they can't, you lose uniqueness, you lose innovation, you lose people who can think on their feet, have that inner drive. Australian cricket has become very dogmatic. At the time when the game is showing all these different ways to succeed, we've become more linear, narrow.

In particular, there was evolving one preferred way to progress. In 2015, the NCC rolled out the apotheosis of the Australian Cricket Pathway, "to create a direct pathway from grassroots to the Australian team", except that it didn't: broken into "Foundation", "Talent" and "Elite & Mastery", it looked more like a game of hopscotch. It offered "high performance experience" to cricketers as young as 12; it scaled soaring heights of banality ("In addition to cricket skill—determination, decision-making and positive self-management are important elements of a players [sic] make up and are a key focus at this stage. A greater emphasis is placed on the ability of the player to demonstrate both the physical and mental skills required"); yet an NCC coach told one startled former Test star that within three years the pathway would obviate the need for a Sheffield Shield.

It is hard to quibble with a system designed and run—in all sincerity—to nurture young talent. Yet there exists a widespread feeling that the plush exclusivity of the pathway is just as likely to offer the worst of both worlds: favouritism to the player on the right side of the velvet rope and on-going discouragement to one on the wrong side, in order to reinforce a coach's initial judgement. As a former Test cricketer, coach and official put it to me:

> For 100 years there was a vibrant club system in Australia, where some players were picked for their state at 17, some at 26, because cricketers mature at different rates. Now it's demanded that everyone looks the same. You'll get a kid who's young, can't hit it far but has a good technique, and who will probably make a cricketer. But he'll get relegated to club cricket, frozen out, because he's not in the pathway and because the coach will be under pressure to justify their original choice. A Mike Hussey would never have succeeded.

A Smith and a Warner, however, might have—which perhaps is the point. By this stage they were more than Australia's captain and vice-captain: stuffed with cricket since their mid-teens, primed, protected and promoted, they were what the system aspired to replicate.

The system was beginning, furthermore, to reach down. In July 2017, the NCC hosted its first conference of coaches from first-grade clubs, who gathered to be inducted in philosophies of the "war for talent" and of "pick and stretch"—a belated attempt to induct those maligned 'clubbies' increasingly sidelined by pathways cricket. A hundred coaches were dinned with the need to identify the cream of 13- to 16-year-olds, the type that "keep the game moving", and Greg Chappell's well-worn dictum about talent being like fruit, needing to be picked when ripe.

FACT: every member of the team that won the 2015 World Cup final had made their first-grade debut by the age of 19.

CONCLUSION: They became star cricketers through being picked at 19.

ALTERNATIVE HYPOTHESIS, NOT CONSIDERED: they were picked at 19 because they were good enough, and that the grade system already effectively recognised them as such without the need to be taught to suck eggs.

PERMISSIBLE INFERENCE: CA believes that the club, built over generations and sustained by all ages, is concerned with nothing more than providing feed stock for the system. "Everything was framed in terms of elite success," recalled an attendee. "You might help build a guy who loves cricket, becomes a terrific club player, plays 250 games, becomes a coach, or a president, or a secretary, spends 30 or 40 years in the game … and the system would call that a failure. They'd only ever be 'a clubbie'."

At Brisbane, the word was "Pathway"; at Jolimont, the two words sewn together were "OneTeam". The organisational transformation bequeathed to Roberts had started humbly as an endeavour to squeeze savings from shared services and amalgamating IT platforms.

Gradually it evolved into what felt to some like an attempt to reduce state associations to branch offices, involving demoralising teleconferences in which project lead Belinda Clark would admonish association staff for using the word 'you' when they should be saying 'we' while management consultant Sean Faehrmann of Nucleus, clocked up billable hours "uniting and aligning Australian Cricket". Opinion divided about the exercise. Some thought it a worthwhile opening of two-way communications; others that it quashed local initiative, and became about "more work for no additional money while CA people stood over you telling you your job".

The paradox here was that the state associations had never been in more constant competition, the ante in domestic cricket having been hugely upped. Never mind "OneTeam": Cricket NSW was now preparing and fielding no fewer than eight teams, the men's Blues in the Sheffield Shield, Matador Cup and Futures League, the women's Breakers in the National Cricket League, and the male and female Sixers and Thunder in the respective Big Bash Leagues all competing for coaches, medical staff, equipment and time even as the future of CNSW's facilities at the Sydney Cricket Ground were clouded by the rebuilding of Allianz Stadium. The CEO meeting these challenges was Andrew Jones, the sharp-minded strategist who had played a part in creating them, and who, in his sometimes volatile responses, did not always engender deep affection.

Whatever OneTeam's accomplishments, it retained a political character. In December 2015, for example, CA's Tasmanian-based director Tony Harrison accused the "fat cat bureaucrats" seeking to obtain a Test match for Canberra of indulging what was "hardly 'OneTeam' behaviour": "We [CA] spent a lot of money and effort getting this OneTeam thing going, and here, instantly, we have an issue." At least he got the "we" right. OneTeam also assumed a particular significance as a means of Roberts showing his management chops, auditioning essentially for the role of Sutherland's successor. His growing prominence in CA was reflected in the departures of two executive general managers in 2016: in July, Kate Banozic left her finance post, after 16 years at CA, to join Endota Spa; in October, operations chief Mike McKenna finally obtained a CEO title of his own at Perth's Optus Stadium, taking his lieutenant Chris Loftus-Hills. Roberts had a setback when his hand-picked head of HR, Anthony Allen, left abruptly. But Roberts won a powerful advocate in new chairman David Peever.

Peever is a banker's son from Charters Towers who spent 27 years at the mining house Rio Tinto, also slotting in seasons of first-grade cricket in Brisbane, at Eastern Suburbs. He now divides time between Melbourne's Brighton and the Sunshine Coast's Maroochydore. He is a corridor operator rather than a limelighter, and initially earned kudos for backing CA away from the unpopular 'Big Three' reforms at the ICC. But his background also drew attention in the context of CA's forthcoming industrial negotiation—in popular imagination, Rio Tinto is associated with environmental despoliation and labour skirmishings. Looking into the new chairman's background for *Cricinfo*, Daniel Brettig quoted from a speech at a mining conference where Peever had expressed a preference for "direct engagement between companies and employees" without interference from "the shop floor" and "the competing agenda of a third party to extend its reach into areas best left to management". For his trouble, Brettig was chided by public affairs at CA: Peever was not "anti-union"; merely pro-management. When CA and the ACA began circling one another in October 2016, however, there were quickly hints that OneTeam was effectively to be extended—there would be little room, as it were, for a Players' Association as a 'Second XI'.

The parties began negotiations far apart—and stayed that way. The ACA's initial submission, which advocated retention of the revenue share for men and the inclusion in it of women, was received in silence. Nearly two months elapsed before CA replied with its submission, advocating a sharp contraction of the revenue share to a core of male and female internationals and merely salaried employment for domestic players. This was not entirely unexpected. Slightly more surprising was that Sutherland was nowhere to be seen. When the ACA's CEO Alistair

Nicholson suggested a one-to-one without prejudice meeting to establish some common ground, Sutherland advised that the carriage of the negotiations lay with Roberts. Peever insisted publicly that his CEO was far too busy for such distractions as negotiating collective bargaining agreements.

Except that there were scarcely any negotiations to speak of. Instead the parties talked past each other, unbudging, unflinching. Nicholson's advisers, former Labor minister and ACTU Secretary Greg Combet and barrister John Whelan, counselled that nothing would happen before the end of the 2016-17 financial year, when the vast majority of player contracts expired—essentially creating a lockout. CA, in their opinion, would then rely on the players buckling under financial pressure.

They were pretty much dead on. In the lengthy hiatus, every ACA request met with high-handedness and foot dragging, Roberts reading laboriously from scripts. Financial forecasts that CA had in past always tendered promptly were not made available until 11 June, almost nine months after first being requested, and then consisted of three slides. The ACA commissioned its own forecasts, from Justin Jameson at Venture Consulting, a specialist in media rights. Again, their modelling would prove to be dead on.

At the dispute's heart lay a philosophical difference. CA held the players to be "employees", which they certainly resembled in observing set hours, receiving superannuation etc. The ACA saw them more complexly, as producers and product, providers of content and sources of intellectual property, and even as the game's conscience, with a practical knowhow and valuable insights into its fast-evolving conduct.

In the context of the dispute, the players also displayed an unexpected collegiality. Cricket in the last decade has found a kind of embodiment in the annual bazaar of the IPL auction, exalting individual aspiration. But there emerged from Australian dressing rooms in 2017 a residual sense of the common weal—a grasp that the health of the system depended on the strivings of every player in it and not merely the success of a prestigious few. With assistance from executive member Neil Maxwell, who manages Pat Cummins and Josh Hazlewood, the ACA raised a fighting fund to see vulnerable uncontracted players through any hardship, securing advances of $5 million from private backers against $52 million in the so-called adjustment ledger—a portion of the PPP calculated from the difference between forecast and eventual revenues.

The dispute's underacknowledged heroines, meanwhile, were women's captain Meg Lanning and vice-captain Alex Blackwell, who kept their colleagues unified. In a dispute where CA worked every pressure point, trying to split international players from domestic players, then certain international players who were to be offered long-term contracts from other international players, the nexus of male and female players was perhaps the most sensitive, the women having much to gain from CA's initial offer after decades of subsistence existence. With neither fuss nor bother, the women were arguably more solid with the men than the men had ever been with the women.

Having behaved like they had all the time in the world, CA then ran out, hemmed in by three tours scheduled in the year's second half: Australia A to South Africa, Australia to Bangladesh for two Tests and India for five one-day internationals, followed by the Ashes at home. When Usman Khawaja and the Australia A team could not be coerced to take their trip, Sutherland at last joined the negotiation—or what might be better described as the capitulation. In the next nine months, New Zealand Cricket and Cricket South Africa both renewed revenue sharing agreements with their players without any trouble.

This is not the place to rehash the dispute's already heavily-hashed arguments. The revenue share had been a boon to Australian cricket—a robust and readily understood mechanism for reconciling interests that do not naturally align. Criticism of it was also not without force. It had been designed in a different time, long before domestic T20 leagues had diversified player incomes; it's possible it did reward some players in advance of achievement. Yet CA never troubled to make its case publicly.

Peever's hand-picked communications maven, ex-Rio Tinto flack Mark O'Neill, instead ran a stealth campaign, reminiscent of the immortal line of the Test and County

Cricket Board's Alan Smith: "No comment, but you can't quote me on that". The seemingly laudable objective of more for "grassroots cricket" was substantiated by little evidence and no plan whatever. The ACA, an organisation so small it lacks even a receptionist, had the public sphere almost entirely to itself. Who were you going to believe? A stunningly awkward video of Kevin Roberts talking to a camera, or the worldly Shane Watson and straight-as-a-die Simon Katich, the ACA's player liaisons?

To repeat, this was not only about money: it concerned power. It takes little to disturb the equipoise of athletes and officialdom. Their relations contain the scope for all manner of day-to-day ranklings. As we have seen, distrust in Australian cricket had been building up for years over matters of selection, scheduling, the marginalising of the well-loved Shield, and the centralising of high-performance initiatives. Now it boiled over. Touring state dressing rooms to make their case, Roberts and Howard encountered strong resistance, and left behind negative and confrontational impressions. When Sutherland fleetingly broke his silence in May 2017, it was in a letter complaining of the ACA's "reluctance to recognise the necessity of change and innovation as circumstances change", citing as evidence the *State of the Game's* argument for changed BBL scheduling and more recent quibblings over the pink ball: the players were being treated not as fellow agents of change but as obstacles to progress.

Peever then shattered the lock-out's false calm with a

blimpish op ed in *The Australian*. Rather than methodically enumerate the needs of cricket in the community, discuss pressures on sporting infrastructure or local volunteers, and demonstrate why an annual distribution to states of more than $100 million was insufficient to serve future needs, Peever commenced by inveighing against … Greg Combet? The bulk of Australia's male and female elite cricketers were unemployed and he was haranguing … an adviser to the ACA? Suddenly cricket seemed to be refighting 2007's WorkChoices election. Had CA set out to affirm every underlying prejudice about administrators that players have ever entertained, they could hardly have succeeded more totally. *The Australian Financial Review* has never been more popular among cricketers than on the days that waspish Rear Window columnist Joe Aston enjoyed some sport at the expense of Peever and other Jolimont executives.

In the main, the Australian team kept its own counsel throughout the dispute, gathering once in public view at the Coogee Bay Holiday Inn for a briefing from Katich and Watson. The exception to the softly, softly approach was, perhaps inevitably, David Warner.

While Steve Smith held aloof, as befitted an Australian captain, Warner showed again an affinity for the role of 'leader'. Some colleagues found this a little awkward; in domestic ranks, however, there was genuine appreciation of the sentiment that the big boys would not cut and run. Warner's public comments were actually never all that outrageous: "We're not going to budge from the revenue sharing model," he said, "We want equality, and a fair share for domestic and female players. That in a nutshell is what it's all about." Granted it was *his* nutshell, but so what? Although his aside that CA "might not have an Ashes" was received as a threat, it was also a perfectly legitimate inference to draw from the impasse in negotiations. What mattered was Warner speaking at all, which made him both beacon and target.

Rumours circulated of a new vice-captain: the name floated was Peter Handscomb, just as his form tapered. Images of Warner and his Lamborghini made for some luxury porn clickbait in *The Australian*, in which sports editor Wally Mason excoriated "these multi-millionaires in flannel" for "threatening to rob Australian sports fans of the greatest spectacle on our shores, the Ashes"; it may have been the most read story of the furore.

This was in some respects the dispute's most troubling aspect, that it incited at least a proportion of cricket's supporter base to effectively barrack against the national team—a team about which some already felt a certain ambivalence, for their chronic instability, their seeming remoteness and their sometimes grating 'Australian way'. But through 2017, CA seemed perfectly content with having their most valuable assets depicted as overpaid prima donnas.

'The players': although they emerged successfully from the game of the pay dispute, they now faced a series to win with the public.

7

Enough Sorries?

I n August 2017, soon after Australia lost for the first time a Test match against Bangladesh, an email began ricocheting round the inboxes of state and national elite coaching and management. It became known as the "Café in Dhaka" message, from where the sender, Pat Howard, reported composing what he acknowledged was "not a supportive email":

> I am sitting in a café in Dhaka hotel at the conclusion of the first Test loss ever to Bangladesh. I am personally embarrassed and take accountability and happy to accept any criticism that comes our way.
>
> For some of you sitting here in Dhaka you are fully aware of how poor a result this is and you have a material opportunity to address in the next few days. Rightly the system is often judged on the outcomes of

the national team. As you can imagine there are many questions being asked of us, and I think they are fair.

I am reasonably confident that many of the players that have just beaten us would not get a run in any of the state teams.

To the CA Team Performance—When you go home at the end of the day, does what you do actually make a difference? CA spends over $100m on players' wages and teams, all in the effort of producing great national teams. We have failed, you have failed and I have failed and it is not good enough.

So I do not expect you to agree with a few of my observations, but here is my view. To put it in context my starting position is that we have the worst batting average in Asia over the last 10 years, bar none:

1. We have been going to the MRF [Pace Bowling Academy in Chennai] for a long time, it doesn't work.

2. The Sheffield Shield does not produce players to perform in the sub-continent, England or in difficult conditions.

3. I think we have grown and think some of what we do makes no impact or minimal impact on performance. I have no doubt you work hard, but does it make a difference?

4. If you want to be the 2nd spinner for Australia you need to be very accurate, because you are only going to play in Asia. We neither value this skill instead admiring how much a person spins the ball. Bangladesh bowled one over of pace against us and every sub-continent team we play will prepare the same type of pitch—and fair enough.

I am not going to wait for the Ashes to expect more. Higher standards of ourselves means higher standards of those around us. Understand change is coming, pressure is unavoidable and if you are not up to accepting that, you are in the wrong place.

Howard was known for his combustibility. It was widely said that "you only ever hear from Pat when you lose": the coaching staff of the women's team had been chewed out similarly after Australia's defeat in the World Cup semi-final a few months earlier. But this catalogue of veering miscellany, with its characteristically chest-baring opening ("take accountability", "happy to accept any criticism"), mindedness of data ("we have the worst batting average in Asia over the last 10 years bar none") and money ("CA spends over \$100m on players' wages and teams"), soon achieved cult status. Yes, Australia had lost to Bangladesh. So had England earlier in the year. The Tigers had been World Cup quarter-finalists in Australia: they were no longer a pushover. And so much for 'OneTeam', eh? Why was the Sheffield Shield getting the blame while the NCC and those precious pathways were exempt from criticism? One typical response from state level read:

When you surround yourself with people who don't think and the programs you run at the NCC are full of people that don't think you end up with lack of ideas and creative ways to take organisations forward.

When you create a culture within the Australian team where the coaches[sic] egos and status are bigger than the team you are going to have a problem.

> When you support and don't address behavioural
> issues in your team you have issues.

People moved on. Thanks to Warner and Nathan Lyon, Australia squared the series in Chittagong. And Pat was Pat. Exasperating as he was, his directness could be a virtue: the ACA was privately convinced that had Howard rather than Roberts had carriage of the MOU, it would have been resolved in a fraction of the time. But here was an ill omen. As it had been a year earlier after Australia's five consecutive Test defeats, the pressure was again on the system to deliver—in order, largely, to justify the system. And those who would bear the principal burden of that were those with whom CA had spent the previous year at loggerheads: the players.

In fact, they would go a long way to doing it. Against England, the Australians looked like a smooth-running machine, as they regularly do on Down Under's doped surfaces, winning 4-0. Steve Smith and David Warner compiled 1119 runs; Lyon, Mitchell Starc, Josh Hazlewood, Pat Cummins and Nathan Lyon took 87 wickets; Lehmann ended the series with a home record against the old enemy of nine wins from ten starts. The hot gospelling about youth of a year earlier had by now rather died away. By the Perth Test, in fact, all the fresh crop of that Adelaide Test the year earlier had slipped from favour—Handscomb, Renshaw, Maddinson, Sayers, Bird and even Wade. In case of the last, the selectors had cast back to thirty-two-year-old keeper Tim Paine, at the time not even wearing the gloves for Tasmania and who had been contemplating retirement—a choice that would be justified by short-term success, then have unforeseeable medium-term effects. Novice opener Cameron Bancroft made few runs but trained hard, mixed well and stood stoically at short leg, as his coach noted approvingly: "For me, you've got a young guy there learning his craft, he's got a great work ethic, so for me moving forward, end of the day it'll come down to selectors but he's a good young kid, works hard, we're pretty happy with him." Lehmann, of course, was a selector himself and the "good young kid" was 25 years old.

All the same, there was an undertone of concern around the team unit. Warner being Warner was one thing; Warner being encouraged to be Warner was another, and influential on other behaviours. The accusation of a nightclub headbutt on Bancroft by England's Jonny Bairstow was mischievously manipulated; the abuse that Warner heaped on England's Tom Curran during the Boxing Day Test was needless and shabby. It wasn't only outsiders uncomfortable with Australia's deportment under Smith and Lehmann. Yet winning blessed everything. CA veritably wallowed in it. After the Sydney Test, the home team received acclaim from a mobile podium where a giant cut-out Ashes was flanked by inflatable hands, one in Australian colours holding up four fingers, the other in English colours clenched to signify zero. "The effect was about as charming as a pneumatic cow pat," observed

The Age's Greg Baum. "But, heh, we've got the Ashes, so stfu England." The players were furious. Even Howard was mortified. And everyone was tired.

In January 2014, I watched Mitchell Johnson and Ryan Harris ascend a less eye-gashing podium after helping administer a 5-0 defeat to England. They were triumphant; they were about to celebrate; they looked like two old diggers shakily ascending the steps at the Shrine of Remembrance. A five-Test series is a brutal contest, perhaps the severest but one—and that one is getting up to play immediately afterwards. Five days after putting those inflatable hands behind them, Smith, Warner, Paine, Cummins, Starc and Mitchell Marsh turned out for the first of five one-day internationals, which they would lose to England 1-4.

Warner had then to lead Australia in a six-match T20 triangular in New Zealand—Howard's initiative, partly to bring Warner back in from the cold at Jolimont, where some directors still seethed privately about him. Warner did the job well, undefeated, again impressing onlookers with his cool deliberateness in the runaway format. Except that it was not for cool that Australian cricket looked from Warner. He was needed, it was felt, to be up and about, introducing some of that 'Australian way' in the upcoming series in South Africa—as indeed he had four years earlier.

About the Australians, instead, there were signs of

distractedness. Smith had been dropping catches, a hint of wavering concentration; Warner was in a white ball fug as a red ball date loomed, a result of poor preparation. The first training sessions in South Africa were listless. How were players rating their fatigues? What were they reporting in their K10s? They had been on the road more or less since mid-August in Bangladesh, and it was now March of the following year. They were about to take on one of the world's strongest teams in the most hostile of environments. Faf du Plessis's Proteas had also been toiling hard, sustaining several injuries in getting the better of India. But South Africa was at home—a status which these days seems to give every host something like a one-Test head start.

At Durban's Kingsmead, the Australians threw themselves into the First Test. They insisted that the pitch microphones be muted; they focused on the fearsome but volatile Kagiso Rabada, who, under the ICC's new code of conduct, was only one minor transgression away from suspension; they were devastating with the ball, Mitchell Starc at his reverse swingingest, and minatory in the field, Warner running out AB de Villiers at an inflexion point in South Africa's second innings with a flash of inimitable brilliance.

He rejoiced with a further flash of inimitable boorishness, berating de Villiers's partner Aiden Markram for an errant call, as Nathan Lyon cheekily dropped the ball by the prostrate de Villiers. The afternoon took on a mano e mano tone. As Markram put on 147 in 204 balls with Quinton de Kock, Warner did everything expected, assailing the latter with whatever came into his head, which wouldn't stretch any imagination far. It's possible De Kock complained to the umpires, as a boundaryside effects microphone at tea caught Warner referring to him as a "fucking sook." It's known that De Kock and Warner had an altercation in the stairwell soon afterwards because it was recorded on CCTV, and watched that evening by ICC referee Jeff Crowe with the captains and team managers —and had it not been for the interposition of teammates and the captain's insistent tug, Warner may have had more to answer for. All because of ... 'the line'. De Kock had apparently made a distasteful sotto voce remark about Warner's wife Candice and a 2007 incident at Sydney's Clovelly Hotel with rugby star Sonny Bill Williams.

Inevitably, the footage was leaked, to South Africa's *Independent Media*. The Australians' hard-won victory was overshadowed by Warner's machismo, and Crowe's financial and point penalties. Sutherland was sufficiently disturbed to speak to Smith, and also to manager Dovey, from Melbourne, stressing his unhappiness: he was astonished that Warner had escaped sanction for his initial barrage at Markram. In public, he took a quieter line, issuing a press release expressing disappointment ("CA reminded the team of the standards of behaviour expected of players representing Australia"), while being critical of both teams' disrespectful attitude to their opponents ("Unfortunately neither team met this standard in Durban"), and standing by the Australians' reputation ("Australia has always prided itself on taking a highly competitive approach to international cricket"). The point was further blunted by a familiar proposition, that Australia's record for ICC code of conduct transgressions was not appreciably worse than anybody else's—it was at least ironic from the country fixated on seeking number one status to be so content to lie in the middle of the conduct rankings.

If the Australians' sorry-not-sorry justifications were a measure, moreover, Sutherland's message hardly penetrated. On the field before the incident, insisted Paine, "cricket stuff" had been the only subject matter ("We were trying to make it an uncomfortable place for Quinton to bat, no doubt, but we didn't cross the line"); in the stairwell, claimed Lehmann, Warner had been within his rights ("When it crossed the line he defended his family and women in general, so from my point of view I thought he did the right thing"); in the future, Warner stated, he wouldn't be changing ("I play with aggression on the field and I try not to cross that line and it has been in the past that I have sort of been fiery, but I don't think whatsoever there on the field that I have ever crossed that line"); in the future, a little more tentatively, Smith took a leaf from a superseded CA strategic plan ("It's about continuing to play a good, hard, aggressive brand but knowing we don't want to cross the line, we want to stay within the spirit of the game and let cricket be the main thing on show").

When the Second Test began at Port Elizabeth, there developed even a measure of sympathy for the players due to the unsparing viciousness of South African spectators, who if 'the line' existed for crowds would well and truly have crossed it. Warner, inevitably, was the main target; Lyon and Starc also had to cop it sweet. Worse, two imbecilic Cricket South Africa officials posed for photographs with fans wearing masks bearing the face of Sonny Bill Williams. In the race to the bottom, it was now South Africa's turn to roll out the sorry-not-sorries.

As Smith had wished, cricket was the main thing on show in a scintillating Test that South Africa won, but it was not the only thing. The Australians looked increasingly besieged, unsure where to bowl to the irrepressible de Villiers, confused whether to stick or twist against the rampaging Rabada. When he bowled Warner, Rabada let loose a tirade; when he trapped Smith, he brushed the passing batsman's shoulder. This very nearly resulted in the code of conduct penalty on Rabada the visitors had hoped for. But after a week of South African legal histrionics, an appeal to the ICC cancelled a suspension that would have been well-deserved: a train wreck of a ruling, which Smith actually did well to forbear. All of which conduced to an air of embattlement and grievance as the tour moved to Cape Town, a city long on crime, short on water, best known for a prison, and vociferously behind a team seeking their first home series win against Australia in nearly half a century. In the Third Test, the Proteas took steady then inexorable control. And at around 3pm on the Third Test's third day, umpires Llong and Illingworth beckoned Cameron Bancroft.

There was no excusing it. It was as crass as Boris Onischenko's *épée*, the Harlequins' blood capsules. The underarm ball of 1981 had at least been explicitly legal; by introducing a foreign object to the degradation of the ball, sandpaper violated both statute and spirit. Sure, it's a grey area. Sure, the game has winked at it. But Australian cricketers do know the difference. In his 2016 autobiography, Mitchell Johnson recounted indulging in lots of experimentation at training: "I rubbed it on concrete and loaded it up with spit just to see what would happen, but I could never do it in a game. I felt like I was doing something illegal when I did that." Because he would have been.

Yet the unedifying truth is that Australian cricket had existed for some time in the realm of whatever it takes. It had told itself that the game was tough, that failure was not an option, and that lengths gone to were all-but immaterial. *'Be relentless … play to win.'* The ball had to be got reversing. A discretionary chafe on the keeper's gloves; saucering the ball in so that it bounced on rough parts of the square; as long as there was no infringement detected of the ICC code of conduct, which Sutherland had just emphasised again was the benchmark of compliance, then what of it? "That's just the way the game goes," Lehmann had said in reference to ball management 'techniques' a few weeks earlier. "I have no problem with it. Simple."

Not any more. All three conspirators tried at first to evade their responsibilities in varying degrees; interestingly, while Smith and Bancroft pled guilty to the ICC, Warner was never charged. But there soon emerged an expectation of exemplary justice, over and above that required by the various laws and codes. There was a strong sense that the public had been awaiting an incident around which to express a generalised dissatisfaction, with the game as well as the team, and were now drawing their own version of 'the line'.

'Confess and avoid', which had first looked so promising a strategy, became unsustainable. Sutherland was aggrieved by a press release from the Australian Sports Commission chair John Wylie encouraging CA to stand down Smith; Peever found it harder to ignore a call from the Prime Minister. Malcolm Turnbull stepped in not once but twice, first to demand "decisive action" against the tamperers ("How can our team be engaged in cheating like this? It beggars belief."), then the next day to insist that "a game that is synonymous with a fair go and fair play" be restored to sanctity; ("I think there has to be the strongest action taken against this practice of sledging. It has gotten right out of control. It should have no place.") 'The Australian Way' was suddenly un-Australian.

The chief aggravating feature was the drafting of Bancroft as the agent of Warner at the discretion of Smith—leading to a cry of 'they-threw-the-kid-under-the-bus'. Yet the 25-year-old 'kid' had played 76 first-class matches in five countries, and got on by a "great work ethic" that included doing jobs others shrank from like going under the helmet at short leg: Bancroft would cheerfully have thrown himself under any bus in the vicinity.

Warner? Well, that'd be right. The episode brought to the fore every hang-up about him—that if there was trouble, he would be nearabouts.

Smith? Et tu, Smudger? But had he not appeared too youthful and too wholesome for a job so onerous as Australia's captain, like a boy who'd found a baggy green in a drawer, and was trying it on in the mirror? His weight could now be seen as of runs rather than of character.

The sponsors, institutional and personal, now queued up to display their piety, although more truly to detach from reputations and brands worth less than when their deals had been signed. Funds management firm Magellan took the opportunity to walk away from a Test match-naming rights deal after the first of three years, when it had only wanted one year in the first place. The Commonwealth Bank washed its hands of Steve Smith, laughably scrubbing away a speck from the general filth of its corporate name. Hypocrisy had a field day. The Rajasthan Royals and Sunrisers Hyderabad dropped Smith and Warner respectively, although the former had just paid

$3 million for the services of a man on an affray charge after a drunken punch-up at a Bristol nighthaunt.

The speed of events and the unanimity of response caught most unawares. Officialdom was coming to the end of a long season too—the summer's last game, the Sheffield Shield final, was in progress at Allan Border Field. Attention was trending down—it had rapidly to be turned up. CA's chairman was in the air on the way home from South Africa as the story broke. CA's chief executive was asleep in leafy Kooyong when a text arrived from his old confrere Michael Brown, who advised that he might want to turn on his television. Pat Howard awoke to discover a bunch of missed calls from manager Dovey, watched footage of the press conference, and immediately booked a flight to South Africa, on which he would be joined by CA's integrity officer Iain Roy. Alistair Nicholson, who had been with the team in Cape Town until the previous day, was on the back of a safari truck on the Botswana border taking a family holiday when his phone, which his wife had admonishingly told him not to turn on, began pinging. His flight on a tiny chartered plane was through a violent electrical storm—while a media storm awaited of an intensity few could remember.

A year earlier, Tim Paine had had one foot out the door, and been weighing up a job at cricket equipment manufacturer Kookaburra. Now he was named Australia's 46th Test captain. There were harrowing scenes as Smith, Warner and Bancroft, constrained by their bans from wearing their CA gear, returned to Australia to display contrition and make expiation. As they fronted the media, only Bancroft had any official support. The Western Australian Cricket Association's thoughtful CEO Christina Matthews sat beside him—many mistook her for Bancroft's mother—while state coach Justin Langer and team psychologist Matthew Bergen were also on hand.

Smith, who flew direct to Sydney, arrived at 5pm, and was decanted straight into a teary press conference at the airport; Warner, unable to obtain seats for his wife and daughters on a direct flight, had to wend his way home via Dubai, arriving in early morning to run a weary gauntlet, waited a few days to consider his options, then faced a media scrum at the SCG alone. There was a solid legal argument that the process had been opaque and the suspensions were excessive. But who would dare challenge it? An overdeveloped sense of employment legalities had entangled AFL coach James Hird during Essendon FC's supplements scandal five years earlier, and it had done him no good. Once Smith and Bancroft had accepted their bans, Warner could only grimace and bear it.

Roy's investigation cleared Lehmann of direct knowledge of the ploy, but drilled no deeper into attitudes regarding the pushing of limits and the stressing of standards. How far ball management had gone previously and who might know were left for later dates. It was hard enough to keep pace with what was in front of one.

In the space of three days, CA dismissed questions about Lehmann's future as "speculation", the coach himself insisted that he was "not going to resign" because he had "no prior knowledge" of the plot, then that it was "only fair" he go because he was "ultimately responsible for the culture of the team". Lehmann's tenure ended amid the debris of a 492-run defeat at Wanderers. A month later, it was announced that he would be seeing out his contract with a sinecure at the NCC: "Lehmann to work with future stars", reported *cricket.com.au*, as it is wont to. There has been huge fascination since with if, when and how the players will return to the colours, surprisingly little about Lehmann's future.

Chairman Peever got so busy, meanwhile, that he overlooked a meeting request from Armando Nuñez, president of CBS Studios International, owner of the Ten Network, CA's broadcast partner in the BBL and then hoping to continue the relationship in a joint television rights bid with the Nine Network. Following up, Nuñez received a withering email response: "Unfortunately your team has completely messed this up. I expected much more given our discussions and the unique position we were affording 10. Franky [sic], the tactics are appalling on a number of levels." CA believed that the joint bid was non-compliant under the terms of its tender; Peever opined that Ten were "not prepared to challenge their operating model to be anything other than bottom feeders in this market."

Like the footage of the skirmishing Warner and de Kock, the exchange became public. After all, whatever the status of the bid by Ten, this was the same network whose sharp and fun coverage had been instrumental in the BBL's success over the preceding five years; it was also a potential on-going broadcast partner. A subordinate sending such a message would have been sidelined from further discussions, if not terminated. Peever lightly excused himself: "I made an apology to the executive in question for the tone of the email ... and that apology was accepted. But it was in the context of a negotiation".

The context of Steve Smith being a young man in a punishing job in a tight corner at the end of a gruelling season had been deemed irrelevant to his lapse of judgment; his older, presumed wiser chairman dealing with a relationship that might be worth a billion dollars to the game sailed blithely on. Peever even said so. At the same press conference, where he foreshadowed reviews of the Australian cricket team and of Cricket Australia, the chairman confirmed not only that Sutherland's position as CEO was "not in question" but that he personally was staying as chairman for three more years—a curiously pre-emptive insistence before the reviews had even begun. His tone, moreover, was of business as usual: "My message to not only the three players but the Cricket Australia staff and those involved in Australian cricket is it is a very sad event and there have been a lot of sorries said. But enough sorries".

J ust as the events in Cape Town provided something of a comment on the culture of the Australian dressing room, so the response to it offered insight into the mindset at Jolimont. The reviews aspired to an "independent" status that immediately came into question. Neither facilitator, Simon Longstaff nor Peter Collins of the Centre for Ethical Leadership, were arms-length appointments: CA director Michelle Tredenick sat on Longstaff's Ethics Centre board; CA had for years used Collins to run in-house seminars. Sutherland popped up the following week to spruik CA's new broadcast partners, Seven and Foxtel, having agreed to a recessing of one-day internationals and some Big Bash League matches behind a subscription wall. The atmosphere was now of bonhomie. Money always puts folks in a good mood.

Ten, Sutherland now acknowledged carefully, had made "an extraordinary contribution" to the success of the BBL; but Ten was also bitterly unhappy about the conclusion of the negotiations, which it had left feeling it had a deal, only to find itself gazumped essentially while executives at CBS International were asleep. There remains adamance on both sides of this disagreement. Ten feels, strongly, that it was misled; CA, with equal sincerity, do not. Whatever the case, the toast was now not so much cricket as money. CA celebrated the price tag, which was $1.18 billion. Seven's CEO Tim Worner celebrated the commercial breaks, whose status as "the most valuable 30 seconds in Australian marketing" would "help define our brand". Promised Worner: "We don't go into these things without a plan, and we have a plan to monetise the sport." Everyone smiled.

On 5 May, Sutherland introduced new coach Langer, to general approval, divulging in the next breath that the coaching search had extended no further than these shores because "the top half dozen coaches in the world are Australian". On 6 June, Sutherland himself bowed out, to respectful tributes, announcing that he had given twelve months' notice after 17 years at the helm. Now it was Peever who, in his discussion of a successor, struck another discordant note:

> What we must do is find the best person for the role. In order to do that we must build the most competitive field in the process to select from that we can. So, while I don't want to put any constraints around it, it is a Cricket Australia role, so we're probably going to have a little bit of a bias towards an Australian, and it is a role in cricket so we're probably going to have a bias towards someone of cricket. But again I don't want to put constraints around that.

Chairman, you just did.

Sutherland, the great survivor, was departing with the thanks of a grateful, far larger and wealthier game, which reaches—and employs—a great many more people, female as well as male, than when he began. He presents an interesting study in the nurturing of innovation and change. The mantle of 'pioneer' or 'visionary' hardly seems to suit his buttoned-down demeanour; perhaps it's more that by his 'steadiness and longevity he enabled change around him. The old board had always been spooked by the threat of an overmighty executive; Sutherland's considered approach and personal decency was instrumental in their staged surrender of powers. Sometimes when the task required more than a process, when the call was for leadership rather than management, when the needs were more intangible than measurable, his limitations had been more obvious, and the duration of his tenure became an impingement on the next executive layer and on general organisational vitality.

Sutherland's views on coaches and Peever's on executives also signified something of a change over the decade. In 2010, cricket had responded to its challenges by looking beyond its ranks; in 2018, cricket was meeting a crisis by closing ranks. One is not necessarily worse than the other, any more than going upstairs is worse than going downstairs. But here they seemed to reflect different stages in CA's life cycle, a transition from an eagerness to ask questions to a presumption of already holding all the answers.

The world does not stand still. An organisation, even in crisis, must go on making decisions, appointments, commitments. Yet one now detected in administrative circles a need to justify decisions already taken—indeed to reinforce and to magnify them, whether this entailed Bigger Bash Leagues, or more day-night Test cricket, or a larger National Cricket Centre, or a more primrose pathway. We're Cricket Australia. We know best. Others envy us. We created cricket. There was nothing here when we began. The players should stay on message or shut up. The sponsors should get down on their knees to us—as one was apparently told recently.

It's not even a particular pride in cricket, but the arrogance of wealth and privilege. In this there feels decreasing scope for cricket to exist organically, spontaneously, joyfully. Rather is effort directed to accommodating the game to the pre-set corporate goals, so that it may take on its allotted and commodified meanings: Test cricket as vestigial tradition (although CA would like it to be four days, and played at night where possible), Sheffield Shield as routine match practice, Big Bash League as mass market entertainment, Futures League as research and development, etc.

Increasingly prescriptive approaches to selection and talent management are in some ways a cognate of these attitudes. Cannot hit the ball to kingdom come? Cannot bowl 140 clicks? Over 25 and haven't played international cricket because you're a keeper and vacancies are so scarce? Sorry, we'll be moving you on. The system requires it. Hang about, what's that? Football clubs are chasing you? Why didn't you say so? Sign here to enlist in the "war for talent" (it's faintly amusing, by the way, how many people in Australian cricket, quite unconsciously, refer not to the "war for talent" but the "war on talent", perhaps echoing the "war on drugs" or "war on waste"—a Freudian slip perhaps).

But here's the thing. For all Australia's manifold advantages, of wealth, resources, heritage, space, climate, standard of living, lock on summer, at the moment we're actually not that good. We were the tough guys; we did headbutt the line; other people were scared of us. They weren't, actually.

The external impression of us is of a team with a good first-choice attack trying to cover brittle batting and shallow reserves with a patina of macho bullshit—good front runners, but, overseas especially, often a bit robotic. At the time of writing, in what is not actually a strong period in the international game, Australia ranks a long way off the pace: third in Test cricket, sixth in one-day cricket, third in T20 cricket. Batting ranks are especially thin, with no available batsmen in the top 20 of the ICC Test rankings, and only Aaron Finch and Travis Head at the lower end of the one-day top 20. David Warner, Steve Smith and Usman Khawaja all emerged ten years ago and more. Who since? Our best equipped young batsman, Matthew Renshaw, was born in England. For all the lavish investment and plenteous opportunity, this decade has arguably been the leanest for batting talent in Australia's history. Would Jason Sangha and Will Pucovski not have emerged anyway, without their sedan chair ride, and perhaps in the process have learned something about self-reliance and self-directedness? Had Pucovski not been pitched into first-class cricket aged 18, would he already have been concussed twice in two years?

Nor does there appear all that much beyond the horizon. In the under-19 World Cup final earlier this year, the gap in quality between the top orders of Australia and India yawned.

Nor is it obvious how such a system might renew itself, even assuming an interest in doing so. Seven years after Don Argus hammered away at the idea of "accountability", the accountability of CA itself has never been less clear. At least in 2011, directors answered to their associations; yet today, with the efficiently "OneTeamed" associations increasingly answerable to CA, directors are virtually in the position of monitoring themselves. There is no equivalent of the inner contention that the clubs continue to nurture in the AFL as being a counterweight to the power of the AFL Commission. There is nothing very much at all.

CA's once-discursive annual report has shrunk in proportion to the growth in its revenues, amounting now to little more than statements from its chairman and CEO back-ended with none-too-detailed financials. There are no regulators to appease, no tax to pay, no government to answer to. Comms staff, while perfectly able, are engaged as much by keeping information in as letting it out: new executive general manager, public affairs Karina Keisler joined at the end of August from the National Broadband Network. She can't be accused of ducking tough assignments.

On 4 May, for example, CA lost its most distinguished

director, Bob Every, late of Wesfarmers, disgruntled with Peever, branding as "sub-standard" the chairman's performance in the pay dispute, the broadcast negotiations and Sutherland's drawn-out succession: it eluded Every in the circumstances how Peever could be supported for consecutive terms as chairman, an honour not even enjoyed by Sir Donald Bradman. CA did not acknowledge Every's resignation until a prod from *The Financial Review's* Joe Aston, which prompted a pro forma press release and a tiny item on *cricket.com.au*.

Whatever the whys and wherefores, Every's exit further illuminated a weakness besetting CA's governance as it is constituted under the "independent board"—that it is supremely difficult to change. In theory, as we have seen, CA is owned by the state associations, and answerable to them; in practice, and increasingly so, those state associations rely on CA for their funding and strategic direction, at the expense of their local identities and practical autonomy. If change was necessary at the top of Australian cricket, from where would the impetus come? From a seemingly supine board where the chairman sits on the nominations committee? From states neutered by an increasingly centralised system? If neither, who else? Structures unable to reform themselves invite interest from outside. Commercial partners already have a strong influence. Might the state, to which CA is actively seeking help to rebuild local cricket infrastructure, want its say? In the event of a Labor government, having a former executive of Rio Tinto as CA's chairman might not play so well.

Four weeks after Every's departure, Jolimont lost its most experienced legal officer, Iain Roy, who more or less invented the integrity function at CA and who was parachuted into Johannesburg to make sense of the situation's rights but who had been at odds with the bureaucracy for some time. Roy's departure came days after Al-Jazeera had presented the gleanings of a year's investigation into *Cricket's Match Fixers*, which Sutherland had waved away with the comment: "Australian cricket is proactive with its sports integrity management." Indeed, general counsel Harman now proactively offered Roy a redundancy and had him leave the same day, even as his integrity off-sider Abhi Arunachalam moved to a commercial role with the Big Bash League. This time CA made no comment and *cricket.com.au* published nothing.

On the employment front, in fact, 2018 has not been a banner year for CA: heads of marketing and communications have left; a group of dedicated staff was restructured out of game development in May by its new executive general manager Belinda Clark; Angela Williamson, a government relations manager for Cricket Tasmania was axed in June by acting executive general manager, public affairs Grant Poulter, for tweeting about abortion rights in Tasmania.

In the latter case, taken to the FairWork Commission by Williamson amid great publicity in July, CA seemed to have nobody capable of explaining their position in public, their CEO being in caretaker mode as the search for his successor continued, their chairman receding again to invisibility. There were certainly no details of these matters on *cricket.com.au*, instead busy reporting such items as that Sutherland, Howard, Justin Langer and Tim Paine were to undertake a study tour of the US to further their "elite learning". From behind Jolimont's walls emanate the sounds of regular restructuring, jarring announcements, awkward interaction. Staff at a recent "drinks with the directors" session described it as "like a Year 9 social". But hey, thousands of people want to work in cricket. Don't they?

Can't argue with a billion dollars, eh? At the end of the day's play, it is this that shores the system up: it delivers financial outcomes. Cricket has been able to harness the ambitions of a driven CEO in Seven's Tim Worner and the hopes of a football-centric subscription television service to slow its off-season churn in Foxtel, so everything is rosy, the reviews will be nodded to, and … oh, look, there's a cricket game. "Enough sorries," to quote the chairman.

Yet other empirical measures of cricket's robustness are rather more disquieting. Australian Sports Commission data published last year about participation in physical activities showed cricket 12th among adults and ninth among children; among adults and children, it wasn't in the top five club sports. Market research done for CA last summer even before Cape Town confirmed fading interest in and passion for the game—and this in an Ashes summer when interest and passion have generally surged. The decline was most marked among women, and in the 45-64 age bracket—a hint of unease among those to whom rankings mean less than reputation. Over the last five years the proportion of adults nominating the Australian cricket team as their favourite national sports team has faded from around a quarter to about a fifth.

In constituencies of traditional strength, meanwhile, there is an undertone of pessimism and puzzlement. Why does the Australian team feel so distant and unappealing, and the honour of representing the country so diluted? Why does the Australian season feel so frantic, and the hierarchy of importance so confused? When did cricket cease to be a complex, skilful, collaborative endeavour of competing team cultures, and decide to be about the identification and pampering of individuals? When did it stop being a game, and become an event, a product, a sale? Are 24 more Big Bash League matches in 2018-19 than in 2016-17 what 'the people' want, or what Jolimont wants them to want?

I hear these somewhat despairing sentiments a great deal. In response, I strive for optimism. A rich game is better than a poor game, and a big game better than a small game, even if being rich and big have their own particular entailments. Living in unreal, overcomplicated and overwrought circumstances, a decent group of young males in the Australian cricket team is doing its best to maintain semblances of normality. Justin Langer is not to universal taste and has had things exactly as he likes them in Perth, but is a man with sound values, and as such answers certain of the players' needs.

There is much in the wider sphere to be satisfied with too. Cricket is more inclusive, more open and generally more aware and reflective of the country in which it is played. The Big Bash League has shown the possibilities when administrators and players face the same way. To watch a Women's Big Bash League or an All-Abilities match is to be uplifted by the game's inspirational possibilities. Even the exercise of talking over cricket's troubles for *Crossing the Line* has been a reminder of how full the game remains of outstanding people who care passionately for it, and how much it moves, excites and unifies us. As I write these concluding words, I am looking forward to a season at the club where I have played for a quarter of a century as much as ever.

Yet I cannot deny that the big cricket I am engaged in watching and writing about feels less precious, less special, less representative and less part of civic life than it used to; more the property of a commercial and bureaucratic elite puffed up with its own importance. Such sensations are in some degree unavoidable—the outcome of cricket's new scale and wealth, the need to clamour for attention amid the general hubbub. But the consequences of CA's changing without a backward glance have, I would argue, had a host of unforeseen consequences.

When Colin Carter and David Crawford rejected cricket's "uniqueness" in a governance sense, it was intended as a counter to the game's insularity; the subsequent reform became, I suspect, the basis for reaction against any sense of cricket's distinctiveness and institutional significance, an indifference to its past, a neglect of its spirit, and a desperation to bring it into conformity with other sports and even entertainments by those who saw only shortcomings.

As an aside, Australian football has loomed way too large in cricket's thinking, especially seeing that cricket scarcely features in Australian football's; Australian football thinks way too much about American football, but that is another issue. Occasionally this keeping-up-with-the-Joneses mentality is not unhelpful: the WBBL has been taken far more seriously in Jolimont for fear of the encroachments of AFL Women's. But the "war for talent" is a pernicious, anti-social and creepily capitalist construct. Evidence is overwhelming that it is better and healthier for boys and girls to play a variety of sports for as long as they can, and to choose the sport they like the most—not the one that makes them the best offer.

Sporting organisations in Australia have historically been congregations of enthusiasts for those activities—sometimes to their detriment. Reshaped by social and demographic change, tides in government funding and the influence of directors with business backgrounds, they have assumed more orthodox corporate guises, albeit that their answerability to multiple overlapping stakeholders rather than portfolio, family or state investors has continued to lend them unique characteristics. That begets confusion. Cricket Australia is more blessed than most of its peers, but it is clearer about what it has changed from than to. For all the demotic pretensions of domestic T20, it is possessed by a yen to control or co-opt everything in its reach, every message, almost every thought. For all its not-for-profit status, it is motivated by, and measures its success, in dollars, is stimulated by the most rather than the best. Even on-field performance is no longer an end in itself. It is a corporate driver, an input to the rewards system, a selling point for marketing, and, perhaps above all, a means by which the system may be vindicated. At Jolimont, success has a thousand fathers; failure is the players' alone.

So in Cape Town the players took the fall. Exhorted to win, they strove too desperately. Encouraged by senses of impunity, they took a risk too many. Exhausted by an apparatus that runs them hard, they had a lapse of judgment. Pushed up to the line, they stumbled across it. And cricket sought solace from the idea that here were just three bad boys.

Bibliography

Brearley, Mike, *The Art of Captaincy*, Hodder & Stoughton, Sydney, 1985

Brettig, Daniel, *Whitewash to Whitewash: Australian cricket's years of struggle and season of plenty*, Penguin, Melbourne, 2015

Chappell, Greg (with Malcolm Knox), *Fierce Focus*, Hardie Grant, Melbourne, 2011

Clarke, Michael (with Malcolm Knox), *My Story*, Pan Macmillan, Sydney, 2016

Clarke, Michael (with Joe Aston), *Captain's Diary*, Pan Macmillan, Sydney, 2014

Haddin, Brad, *My Family's Keeper*, HarperCollins, Sydney, 2016

Haigh, Gideon and David Frith, *Inside Story: Unlocking Australian Cricket's Archives*, News Custom Publishing, Melbourne, 2007

Harris, Ryan (with Stephen Gray and Jason Phelan), *Rhino*, Hardie Grant, Melbourne 2014

Johnson, Mitchell (with Peter Lalor), *Resilient*, HarperCollins, Sydney, 2016

Lalor, Peter and Malcolm Knox, *Phillip Hughes: the official biography*, Pan Macmillan, Sydney, 2015

Lehmann, Darren (with Brian Murgatroyd), *Coach*, Penguin, Melbourne 2016

Michaels, Ed, Helen Handfield-Jones and Beth Axelrod, *The War for Talent*, New York, 2001

Ponting, Ricky, *Ponting at the close of play*, Harper Sports, Sydney, 2013

Rogers, Chris (with Daniel Brettig), *Bucking the Trend*, Hardie Grant, Melbourne, 2016

Waugh, Steve, *Out of My Comfort Zone*, Penguin, Melbourne, 2005

SPORTS SHORTS

Upcoming
Sports Shorts titles:

THE LAST FRONTIER — AUSTRALIA IN INDIA, 2001
BY PAUL CONNOLLY

In 2001 Steve Waugh's all-conquering Australian Test cricket team travelled to India in search of their first away series win since 1968. The result was the most fascinating Test encounters of the era, as Waugh, Shane Warne, and Matthew Hayden attempted to overcome history, the country's frailties on Indian pitches, and the brilliant likes of Sachin Tendulkar, VVS Laxman, Rahul Dravid and Harbhajan Singh.

Journalist Paul Connolly was on the spot for the entire series, both as journalist and fan, trained observer and wide-eyed tourist. Having fallen under the spell of a country and a cricket culture that has fascinated so many Australians down the years, Connolly now looks back with older, wiser eyes upon three classic Tests in a sweeping, personal account of a distant time and place.

BRADMAN & PACKER — THE DEAL THAT CHANGED CRICKET
BY DANIEL BRETTIG

In 1977 Kerry Packer's World Series Cricket insurgency jolted a staid and traditional sport into a period of chaos and upheaval. Pitting traditionalists against revolutionaries, and players against their paymasters, the affair forever altered not only the power dynamics of the summer game, but the way in which it was presented and viewed.

Much is now understood of Packer's role in first seizing control of cricket, then handing it back in a drastically different shape, but far less of the part played by Sir Donald Bradman— better known as the game's greatest batsman, but also an administrator of far-reaching, if secretive, influence.

In *Bradman & Packer — The Deal that Changed Cricket*, journalist Daniel Brettig, author of the award-winning *Whitewash to Whitewash*, deftly reconstructs the shadowy period that remade cricket. When two titans of Australian life came face to face in a clandestine meeting, they brokered the peace deal that ended a sporting war.